PRAISE FOR

First Date Stories

First Date Stories

First Date
Stories

WOMEN'S ROMANTIC

AND

RIDICULOUS MIDLIFE ADVENTURES

JODI KLEIN

SHE WRITES PRESS

Published 2021
Printed in the United States of America
Print ISBN: 978-1-64742-185-4
E-ISBN: 978-1-64742-187-8
Library of Congress Control Number: 2021906049

For information, address:
She Writes Press
1569 Solano Ave #546
Berkeley, CA 94707

She Writes Press is a division of SparkPoint Studio, LLC.

Book Design by Stacey Aaronson

All company and/or product names may be trade names, logos, trademarks, and/or registered trademarks and are the property of their respective owners.

Names, identifying characteristics, and locations have been changed to protect the privacy of certain individuals.

Ingrid Berman™ is a trademark of the Estate of Ingrid Bergman

Excerpt from *The Day I Shot Cupid: Hello, My Name is Jennifer Love Hewitt and I'm a Love-aholic* by Jennifer Love Hewitt. Copyright © 2010. Reprinted by permission of Hachette Books, an imprint of Hachette Book Group, Inc.

"New Faces" reprinted by permission of The Joy Harris Literary Agency, Inc.

Excerpt from "New Face" from REVOLUTIONARY PETUNIAS & OTHER POEMS by Alice Walker. Copyright © 1972, renewed 2000 by Alice Walker. Reprinted by permission of Houghton Mifflin Harcourt Publishing Company. All rights reserved.

To Michael, my "Mr. Yes"

Table of Contents

The Story Behind First Date Stories

"How about we get something to eat?" Brad asked as we left the independent bookstore where he'd suggested we meet.

"Sounds good to me," I responded, smiling. I was pleased that he looked like his Match.com photos and that his personal specs—height and eye color—were as advertised. I'd been on too many dates where the man who showed up wasn't true to the guy I previewed online. Brad didn't disappoint.

We strolled down Santa Cruz Avenue, chatting under the early afternoon sun. The conversation flowed nicely. We hit many of the first date standards: hometowns, jobs, weather, sports. I easily kept up with his gait and sensed a slight bounce in my step. It didn't matter that I had no idea where we'd be eating. I'd let my handsome six-foot companion surprise me.

As we approached the local grocery store, Brad veered off the sidewalk. I followed him across the parking lot and into the store, all the while wondering what he could possibly need to pick up. Was he running an errand on our date?

Brad headed directly to the deli counter. I watched him as he leaned down and surveyed the cornucopia of salads and other prepared food on display in the glass cooling case. He stood up and waved over one of the deli assistants. When she approached, he rested his pointer finger against the glass to direct her attention to the mound of premade food in front of him. I stood speechless, my eyes transfixed on Brad's every move.

"Can I taste the corn and chicken salad?" he asked. The clerk handed him a small fork and one bite of salad in a plastic ramekin. He turned to me. "What are you going to taste?"

"Uhhh . . ." I glanced into the case. "I'll try the lentil salad," I replied cautiously.

"She'll have the lentil salad," Brad repeated to the grocery employee, in the familiar manner a man uses when he's ordering for his companion at a restaurant.

The plastic cup with its spoonful of salad remained untouched in my hand as I watched Brad taste his way through most of the items in the display case. I was baffled. Then it hit me: *He's taken me to the grocery store's deli counter to sample food for free for our first date!*

⁓ℯ⌒

Oh, Brad! This "romantic" deli counter outing was one of the more memorable first dates I've been on. I'm a seasoned dater—an alumna of nearly four hundred dates. Dating for decades isn't something that people usually tout. But why not? Isn't it better to wait to meet the right partner than to divorce the wrong one? Many women who reach their thirty-fifth birthday single, or rejoin the dating scene later in life, know that finding enduring love can be tough. The hardest part isn't finding men to go out with. Thanks to that multitalented phone that's probably within arm's reach of you right now, you're likely just one dating app and a series of swipes or thumb taps away from getting a flirtatious conversation going with some guy, somewhere.

But it is incredibly hard to find a man with whom you want to develop a fulfilling relationship—and it's even more difficult to find a man with whom you want to build a life. I should know. I became a master at going on first dates.

The first date is where every relationship begins. The first date is all about detecting a spark, even just a hint of a connection. You may think you've sensed that spark from texts, e-mails, or calls between you and the man who's caught your eye, or from a virtual date that the two of you have had. But you can't be sure. It's only when you're with him in person that you can accurately detect whether or not there's chemistry. All your senses are activated, taking in his presence, level of energy, appearance, body language, and even his personal scent. Your mind is consciously, and subconsciously, in assessment mode.

Do I feel safe with him?

Does he seem nice?

How well does our conversation flow?

Do we have things in common?

Am I attracted to him—his personality, his looks?

Does he make me laugh?

Could I see myself kissing him?

Do I want to spend more time with him?

You get the idea. There are a series of questions that people answer for themselves during and after each date. And there are plenty of additional questions that we have to find the answers to for that first "hello" to evolve into a committed relationship.

I was—and remain—a big believer in the power and necessity of hope. The hope that my next first date would trigger that sought-after spark was one of two things that kept me in the dating world for twenty-six years after college. The other is my deep-seated belief that every woman who wants to be coupled is worthy and deserving of enjoying a lifelong, loving relationship with her ideal match.

My first job after college was in sales. Each day I spent a few hours making grueling cold calls. I was hung up on. I was left on hold indefinitely. But every so often I was able to talk my way into a meeting with a prospect. The deals took months to close. Most of them never did. During my first annual review, I told my boss how frustrated I was to have so many calls end with the word "No." He paused for a moment and said, "Always remember, every no is closer to a yes."

His words have stayed with me ever since. It didn't take me long to realize that his advice applies as much to dating as it does to sales. In many ways, being on a date is like being on a sales call. Both people are trying to figure out if the other one is compatible and, ultimately, whether they're both interested in the same "deal." Depending on the type of committed relationship each person is seeking, the deal could be living with a life partner, getting married, or another arrangement. I know plenty of women who closed the deal and found their "Mr. Yes" before their thirtieth birthdays. Whether those introductions happened in college, through work, via friends, at their places of worship, or some other way, it was relatively easy for them. Some of those marriages didn't last, but most have.

There are other women for whom the "deal" takes a decade, or longer, to close. I call these ladies "seasoned" daters and fell squarely into this category myself. We seasoned daters spend years mostly meeting Mr. No's. Many of these men are pleasant enough, but the spark is never lit.

Most women also meet Mr. Maybe's, men who we're not quite sure about but decide to get to know. Taking that risk is the only way we can figure out if an initial attraction and connection will develop into enduring love. We invest our cherished time, energy, and emotions. For many of us, Mr. Maybe's are the men who we date exclusively and who we may elevate to boyfriend status.

Like me, you may have spent months, or even years, with Mr. Maybe's who you ultimately realized were Mr. No's. I mourned the passing of those relationships, even when I was the one who brought things to a close. It took time to move forward. As awful as the emotional pain was, I had the gift of a better perspective—and hours spent binge-watching Meg Ryan rom-coms —to take away from the breakup. I became clearer on what my "must-haves" in a relationship were, and the behaviors and actions that I wouldn't tolerate. I also grew to better understand how to be a loving, present partner and yet remain uniquely me as part of a couple. I eventually got to a place where I was ready to start dating again.

Through those experiences, I learned that even if I never met my Mr. Yes, I would have a happy and meaningful life. I loved and valued myself enough to walk away from Mr. Maybe's in search of my Mr. Yes. I eventually came to accept that I may never meet him. Perhaps I wouldn't have a man to start and end each day with. Perhaps I wouldn't have a man to snuggle with every night. But I would still feel good about myself. (Not to mention that I'd get all the closet space and bathroom cabinets to myself and could watch whatever I wanted, whenever I wanted, on TV.) Because the truth is, no one needs to be in a romantic relationship in order to enjoy a great, fulfilling life.

What I didn't realize then—and what I know now—is that all the wisdom I was accumulating on date after date with hundreds of Mr. No's and Mr. Maybe's was helping me become Ms. Yes for someone I had yet to meet.

Even when we do come to the realization that we don't need a man to be happy or to feel fulfilled, we may still want someone by our side. Now for some cold reality: as we get older, it becomes harder for us to date at the same pace as we did in our twenties and early thirties. Let's face it. Our days get jam-packed with all sorts of obligations, commitments, and complexities as we move through the stages of life. There are also societal dynamics outside our control that make dating tougher. All of these factors boil down to six Dating Deterrents that aren't often collectively discussed.

DATING DETERRENT #1 - SUPPLY AND DEMAND

The first is supply and demand. The longer any woman spends in the dating scene, the fewer men there are to meet. When a woman is in her twenties, more men in her same age range are single than when she enters her forties, fifties, and decades beyond. It's a simple fact, for better or for worse.

You may be all too familiar with this reality. But don't despair. Men coming out of marriages or long-term relationships get added back into the pool. Yes, some of these men are in rebound mode. Others are so scarred by their marriages that they will date casually but pull away when the possibility of commitment comes into view. I went out with a lot of these men in my forties. Our first, second, and third dates were usually fun, playful, and romantic. But the prospect of additional dates triggered their fears of commitment. They'd pull a Houdini and suddenly disappear.

Fortunately, there are lots of men emerging from relationships who are more mature and self-aware than they were when they got married. Many of these men are likely in tune with the qualities they're looking for in a woman and have a better handle on how to be a part of a giving relationship. Their re-entry into the dating pool raises its caliber.

DATING DETERRENT #2 - LIFE'S COMPLICATIONS

The complications that life serves up as we get older is the second Dating Deterrent. More obligations and commitments arrive with every passing year. Understandably, many of us prioritize our jobs over our social lives. There are mortgages, student loans, and bills to pay. We may have kids or other family members to take care of. Serious health issues of our own can arise, which we need to focus on and overcome. Then there's the ramification of all the personal upheaval and anxieties that the Covid-19 pandemic left in its wake to work through. These, and many more factors, consume the carefree time that we would like to spend socializing, having fun, and meeting men.

DATING DETERRENT #3 – SOCIETAL PRESSURE

All the while, societal pressure is mounting around us—the third Dating Deterrent. Sometimes this pressure is subtle. Most of the time, it's not. There's the relative who blatantly asks, "When are you going to get married?" or the mother who reminds you how much she'd like grandkids. There's your longtime family friend who says, "I wish I had someone to set you up with, but every man your age I know is married." There's the ob-gyn who gently asks if you want to consider freezing your eggs soon.

Sound familiar? These people mean well, but their comments and judgments only make us feel more stressed about finding a lifelong partner. We doubt ourselves and wonder why we haven't met him yet. This pressure is not helpful or healthy. Do your utmost to tune out these comments or let them ricochet off you. Don't allow them to get you down or in any way degrade how you feel about yourself.

DATING DETERRENT #4 – A WOMAN'S AGE

Age is the fourth Dating Deterrent that impacts seasoned and returning daters. We live in a society that celebrates youthfulness over aging and the maturity it brings. Standing in the checkout line at the grocery store, it's impossible to ignore magazine covers promoting articles about how to avoid or slow down the aging process.

Like me, you've probably encountered men who have bought into this cultural preference. I'd always laugh when I read men's dating profiles that listed the ideal woman's age as being fifteen, or even thirty, years younger than their own. Instead of getting angry or frustrated, feel sorry for these men. They are missing out on being with a more mature woman who's more confident in and out of the bedroom, self-sufficient, open to what life might bring, and opts for authenticity instead of playing games.

Thankfully, the ageism Dating Deterrent isn't universal. There are many men who value life experience and want to date women who have plenty of it. These are the men worth spending time getting to know.

DATING DETERRENT #5 – FEAR OF GETTING HURT AGAIN

Sometimes we can get so frustrated with the dating scene, or emotionally bruised by it, that the fear of getting hurt again—the fifth Dating Deterrent—keeps us from dating. But the tough truth is that rejection is required for the dating process to work. Everyone suffers rejection. Either you're rejecting the man or he's rejecting you until the day arrives when you meet your Mr. Yes. There's no shame in this. Don't take it personally! I realize that it's one of the hardest things to do and yet that's exactly what needs to happen.

You're looking for compatibility and so are the men you're

meeting. If you don't hear back from someone, or you're not both feeling it, or the timing is wrong, then you should let go. Sure, you may need to take a break to dust yourself off, but don't allow those goodbyes to prevent you from moving forward.

DATING DETERRENT #6 – COMMUNITY SUPPORT DECREASES

As I remained single, I found the drop in communal support to be the hardest aspect of dating year after year. For me, this final Dating Deterrent was the most difficult one. When I started my post-college dating adventure with the hope of meeting my match, I was part of a community of women living a shared desire. My friends and I would go out together on Friday and Saturday nights to have a good time and meet men. We were each other's "wing-women." We talked about what to wear, listened to each other's date stories—good and bad—and offered our advice and sometimes unsolicited opinions. When friends had their hearts broken, we were there to lift each other up. When friends fell in love and the relationships took off, we'd celebrate together.

By the time I moved into my thirties, the size of that group had shrunk. As I progressed through that decade, my single friends numbered fewer and fewer. While I still had a core group of unattached girlfriends—some of whom were newer friends—by the time most of us were in our midforties, our group had dwindled to just a handful of women. Are you living your own version of my experience? Can you relate?

By the time I reached midlife, dating had gone from being a supportive, shared experience to what often felt like a solo journey. I was happy for my friends who were married or in committed relationships, but most of them no longer had the time to help me get pumped up for a first date, or the dates that might follow, or to debrief afterward. Understandably, they were busy trying to balance their hectic lives with their children, jobs, husbands, and life partners.

Since I didn't have many women to share and compare dating stories with, I looked elsewhere. I couldn't find a place offline, or online, that was for women dating at this age to connect and propel each other forward. Magazine columns and blogs about dating rarely addressed single women in midlife.

I discovered that I wasn't the only person who felt this way. So I began working on *First Date Stories*, this collection of women's real-life dating adventures, from the romantic to the ridiculous and everything in between. I've chronicled these stories so that women—especially those who are in their midthirties and beyond—can read about, and learn from, other memorable debut dates.

It's often through storytelling that we connect and gain guidance, validation, and empathy. Reading other women's tales will help you attain perspective on your own dates. This book exists to entertain, educate, and motivate you. It's here to help you approach your dating journey with confidence and lessen any frustration, or sense of isolation, that may set in.

I want all daters to believe that they will find love, no matter how unlikely it may seem at times. And to do that, you must keep going on first dates. Millions of women just like you are still riding the first date roller coaster. *First Date Stories* will help all seasoned and returning daters take the ride together.

The stories were selected for this collection because together they span the range of outcomes. There are uplifting and romantic stories for you to read just before you get ready to go on a first date. If you go on a mediocre, disheartening, or even dreadful one, there are stories about women who endured equally disappointing, and likely even worse, first encounters. At the end of each real-life story, I've included some hard-won wisdom from the women who shared these tales, dating coaches, and me, all to help you along the path to true love.

Every story was written based on the recollection of the female dater. That I chose to write from the female's perspective should not be taken as a bias against men. This book aims to connect you with other women's experiences. Likewise, that these stories focus on heterosexual daters should not be regarded as purposefully exclusionary of the LGBTQ community. It is my hope that everyone will find the love they seek.

First Date Stories is intended to help propel you onward through your dating journey. I want you to embrace your fabulousness and recognize that you are worthy of love. Whether you're still seeking your match or you're back in the dating world after a divorce, breakup, or the death of someone you loved, you must not get discouraged and swear off dating permanently. Nor should you settle for less than you deserve.

I didn't. For twenty-six years, I believed I would meet my match. Not every hour of every day, but more often than not. I started writing *First Date Stories* a few years before I went on the most important first date of my life—with my future husband. I share with you how he and I met, and the first date we went on, in the book's final chapter. Now I know that all the dating ups and downs that I lived through before meeting him were worth it, even if it didn't feel like it at the time.

I hope that *First Date Stories* will motivate you to continue going on first dates. The reason is simple: if you don't go on a first date, you'll never go on a second, a fifth, a tenth, and move toward a lifelong, loving partnership.

And remember: Every Mr. No gets you closer to Mr. Yes.

"I have learned not to worry about love;
but to honor its coming
with all my heart."

— *Alice Walker*

author and poet

The Eight-Minute Date

*S*tephanie knew that the wide plastic soles on her tan UGG boots were not designed for speed walking, much less a light jog. Still, she tried to move as quickly as possible without risking a fall or perspiring. She was meeting Frank for the first time and didn't want beads of sweat on her brow. Years of experience had taught her that dating is about first, second, and third impressions. She wanted to look her best.

Stephanie didn't regret her choice of footwear. Had she worn her brown leather flats, she would have been at the coffee house at least a minute earlier. But she was sure that her outfit—skinny jeans tucked into the Australian boots and her favorite pink corduroy jacket worn over a cream Splendid T-shirt—was exactly the right look for her date with Frank. After all, they were meeting at Gaylord's Caffe Espresso, where "casual urban chic" was the unstated dress code.

Lots of e-mails had traveled between Frank and Stephanie during the week, but she couldn't remember if she'd told him that it wasn't her style to be on time. All her friends knew it, and they accepted her tardiness. If Stephanie hadn't warned Frank, she knew she risked tainting his first impression of her. But it couldn't be helped. It had taken her longer than expected to decide which scarf and hat to wear. The cream wool set was the eventual winner. Seven minutes late was her standard arrival time. This Sunday afternoon, though, she would be pushing ten.

Stephanie had been eager to meet Frank ever since she read the first Match.com e-mail he sent her. She was flattered that he'd described her as an "exceptional, sexy woman." That they both enjoyed cooking and camping and shared a weakness for crème brûlée made her hopeful that they would find a connection. Frank's profile photos showed a tall, blond man with tousled hair, and he sported the outdoorsy hiker look that she'd been attracted to since college.

His e-mails were friendly and concise, averaging a mere two or three sentences. Since he owned and ran a construction company, she assumed he didn't have extra time to write more. Frank had listed his income on Match at over $250,000. She was sheepish to admit that she pictured him checking his Rolex occasionally while he waited for her.

Stephanie turned the corner onto Piedmont Avenue and walked up to the coffee shop door. Pulling it open, she stepped into the eclectically decorated café. Oil landscape paintings adorned the walls, and an original Ms. Pac-Man video game table sat tucked in a corner. Stephanie scanned the half-full room. On her second pass, she noticed a man seated at a small round table across the café. He stood and, looking at her, did a two-finger wave, the kind one uses to hail a taxi. With his slicked-back, thinning blond hair, starched jeans, and loafers, he looked more like the stereotypical used car salesman than the guy in the photos. She sighed.

"You almost didn't make the cutoff," Frank said as she approached.

"I didn't do what?" Stephanie asked, startled by the brusque greeting. She'd expected a smile and a hello—the usual pleasantries people exchanged when meeting for the first time.

"Make the cutoff," Frank repeated. "You're late."

"Yes, I realize I'm late. Sorry about that," Stephanie said, fidgeting a bit. She felt bad, but what was done was done.

As she pulled out one of the table's wooden chairs, she noticed an empty coffee cup in front of where Frank had been sitting. He remained standing silently as she took off her hat and scarf. Placing them on the table, Stephanie shook her head casually from side to side, coaxing her wavy hair into place. She removed her gray cross-body purse, hung it on the seatback, and put her jacket over it.

"Would you like something to drink?" Frank asked after she'd finished removing her outerwear.

"Yes, I'll take a mocha. Thanks," Stephanie replied, still standing.

"Okay, I'll wait here while you get it," he said, and then sat down.

Her eyes widened in disbelief. Had she heard him correctly? Since Frank was staring back at her with a blank look on his face, she realized that she must have. Robotically, she reached into her purse, pulled out her wallet, and headed to the counter.

Did he balk at buying me coffee to punish me for being late?

He'd been the one to ask her out, so she had assumed he'd pay. It was a gesture that Stephanie appreciated and didn't take lightly. She understood the value of a dollar and spent hers wisely.

Her twenty years working as a nanny had generated a lot of personal satisfaction but not a large income. It had been over two years since Stephanie got a raise. Moreover, she came from a generous extended family, and her parents had taught her that a person's generosity, whether measured in time, talent, or dollars, revealed a lot about what kind of person they were.

Stephanie stopped a few steps in front of the counter.

Should I even bother? I could save the four dollars and just leave. Or I could get a coffee and see where things lead.

She stepped forward and ordered a mocha.

When she returned to the table, Frank took the iPhone that had been consuming his attention and placed it in his back pocket. Stephanie sat down. He leaned forward in his chair and smiled. His teeth were white and straight; the result of braces, she figured.

"Let's try this again. So, what did you do this weekend?" he asked.

"I sailed to Tiburon with some friends," she replied.

"Ah, Tiburon," Frank said slowly, drawing out the words in a way that made Stephanie think that he was reminiscing about a special time spent in the waterfront town. "Did you go to Sam's Anchor Cafe?"

"Why, yes, I did," she answered, scooting her chair forward. "Actually, I love that restaurant." One of her favorite getaways, she'd spent three hours the day before seated on the restaurant's vast deck, enjoying some cocktails while gazing out over the bay.

"Sam's is pretentious. It's just awful," Frank said. Stephanie saw no levity in his brown eyes. He was serious in his indictment.

An awkward silence ensued. Frank stared into his empty coffee cup. Stephanie picked up hers and sipped it slowly.

How much more of this guy's attitude am I going to take?

After what seemed like a minute, but was probably less, Frank looked up and blurted out, "I'm really into antiques. Are you?"

"No, I'm really not," she replied.

"You're not? Why? Antiques are the embodiment of the history of a family, a society, a people," Frank said. "Even though the pieces are old, most of them are stately and mysterious in truly unique ways. I spent a lot of my childhood going to antique flea markets with my mom. It was an adventure each time we went."

As Frank rambled on about why he enjoyed antiquing, Stephanie's mind wandered.

I probably should have saved the four dollars.

Stephanie took another long sip of her drink. It was almost gone.

When Frank stopped speaking, she looked up, leaned back in her chair, crossed her legs, and smiled.

What happened to the connection we had on e-mail? Maybe some flirting will salvage this date.

Frank flashed her a momentary grin but then shifted his gaze to her tan UGGs. He looked down at them intensely.

"Nice shoes," he said in a tone of voice that could only be interpreted as sarcastic.

Stephanie threw her hands in the air. "What? You don't like my shoes?"

"Don't you have any heels?" he replied.

Stephanie could feel her face heating up. She sprung out of her chair. "Listen, buddy, in the eight minutes I've been here you have reamed me for being late, made me buy my own coffee, trashed Sam's after I told you I liked the place, dominated the conversation talking about antiques after I said that I'm not interested in them, and then you insult my choice of shoes! Exactly who do you think you are? And you don't even look like your photos!"

Stephanie yanked her jacket and purse from the seatback, grabbed her scarf and hat, and stormed out of the café without looking back. Testing the speed at which she could move in her UGGs, she turned the corner and walked as fast as she possibly could for three blocks until she reached her apartment building. All the while, she ignored her ringing phone.

When Stephanie got home, she collapsed onto the couch, pulled off her boots, and kicked her feet up onto the cushions. Lying there, she played back all that had happened during her record-setting date.

How could a date that seemed to have so much potential go so terribly wrong?

After a few minutes, Stephanie sat up and pulled out her phone. Frank had called her three times and left a voice mail after the third missed call. Stephanie pressed the "play" button.

"Hi, Stephanie. You should know that you've really opened my eyes to the errors of my ways. I'm going to handle things differently in the future. Sorry about what happened. Take care."

"Good luck with that," she said sarcastically before pressing the "delete" button.

Stephanie reached down, picked up her UGGs, and carried them into the bathroom. Placing them on the closed toilet seat cover, she opened the cabinet drawer and pulled out her suede brush. She first worked on the left boot and then on the right, lightly brushing the nap toward the rear of each boot to restore the smooth grain that had been disrupted ever so slightly.

After inspecting each boot, she carried them into her bedroom and placed them back in their appointed spot on the floor of her closet. They were ready for her next date.

The Rest of the Story

Stephanie and Frank never spoke to or saw each other again.

Dating Takeaway Tips

BE ON TIME.

Even if you're habitually late, do your utmost to show up on time to a first date. It shows respect. It shows interest. It helps the other person feel like you value the time you're going to spend with them. If you *are* late (it can be a tough habit to break), don't wait for them to comment. Immediately upon arrival, smile, make eye contact, and offer a *sincere* apology. Pay close attention to their response, trying to determine if they're an "a little late is okay" kind of person or an "I hate when people are late" kind of person. This information will help for the next date, if there is one. And you'll learn a lot about them by their response to your heartfelt apology.

TRUST YOUR GUT BUT VERIFY.

It's important to listen to what your gut is telling you. It's usually right. The outcome of Stephanie's date would probably have been the same whether she'd left or stayed. However, before going all in on your intuition, remember that the "shazam" moment, where you fall head over heels for a new beau, is what happens in the movies far more often than in real life. Don't expect to get a dopamine buzz within the first few minutes of meeting. Your date's nerves may hinder their conversational skills and prevent them from coming across as their best self. Find the balance between your head and your heart. There may be non-negotiable signs you're picking up right away that indicate they're not a match. If that's the case, move on. However, they might turn out to be a great person who could make you extraordinarily happy, if you'd only give the two of you the chance to get to know each other better. After all, aren't happiness and kindness two of the gifts you're seeking in a life partnership?

OUTDATED PHOTOS COULD BE A WARNING.

Your date may have posted old photos on their profile because they want to promote an image of themselves when they were in the prime of their attractiveness. If they turn out not to look like their profile photos, it's logical that you're going to interpret this misrepresentation as a lie. View this as a yellow flag, not a red one, since you don't know much about them yet. They may have a good explanation for why they haven't posted current photos. It could be as simple as they don't have any. If you get to date two or three, just ask about it. And be cautious early on before fully trusting them. If they are going to misrepresent something that is so easy to uncover as untrue, what other falsehoods might they have in store?

WEAR CLOTHES THAT MAKE YOU FEEL GREAT ABOUT YOU.

Stephanie should acknowledge Frank's feedback and realize that her outfit didn't create the first impression she'd intended it to. She chose to wear a statement piece—the UGGs. It was a risk and it didn't pan out. But she felt great about herself while wearing them, and that helped her walk into the café with confidence. You want to feel the best you can about yourself when you're on a first date. The clothes you select play a part in getting that vibe going. If you wear a statement piece, you must be prepared for your date not to share the same fashion taste as you. But fashion differences can usually be overcome by a cheerful smile and friendly attitude. If your date is a quality person, it will be the woman in the clothes, not the clothes she's wearing, that matters.

"A good place to meet a man is at the dry cleaner. These men usually have jobs and bathe."

— *Rita Rudner*
comedian and author

The Real Jim

"I'm giving him ten minutes more and then I'm leaving," Ellen announced to her bar companions. Her declaration was fueled by the frustration of Jim's tardiness, a festering doubt that he'd show up, and the mojito that she'd nearly finished.

Her new friends at the bar agreed that a thirty-minute grace period was overly generous. "A true gentleman arrives promptly and is there to greet his date when she enters the restaurant," the woman seated next to Ellen declared.

Ellen felt a tap on her right shoulder as she took a sip of her dwindling cocktail. She spun the leather barstool around to see a brown-haired, hazel-eyed man dressed in a well-tailored dark gray suit standing before her. The collar of his light blue dress shirt was white, a color combination that seemed more appropriate for Wall Street than a casual harborside restaurant in Boston. He had salt-and-pepper hair running along his temples, and crow's feet were settling in at the corners of his eyes.

"Hello," he said. "The hostess directed me over to you. You must be Ellen." He extended his right hand. "I'm Jim. It's nice to meet you. Sorry I'm late."

Ellen smiled and shook his hand. "You're right, I'm Ellen. It's good to meet you too. I wasn't one hundred percent sure that you'd be coming tonight."

"Oh, yeah, sorry that I've been incommunicado since we talked three weeks ago," he said. "Between business travel and the nonstop phone calls I'm on with clients, I often forget to make personal calls. And tonight I had a hard time getting an Uber. But we're both here now."

He glanced over at the dining room inside Rowes Wharf Sea Grille. "I don't know about you, but I'm hungry. How about we get a table and order some dinner?"

"Let's do it," she responded, her flirtatious smile on full display.

Ellen slid off the barstool and reached for her purse. She said goodbye to her bar mates and followed Jim to the restaurant's hostess station. As she walked, Ellen's thoughts went to the person responsible for fixing the two of them up. Bart Collins, a family friend, had assured her that Jim was one of the smartest and most interesting men he knew, as well as the sharpest lawyer he'd ever hired. Mr. Collins had a hunch Jim and Ellen would get along well, and she had no reason to doubt it—she trusted that her parents' friend had her best interests in mind. So far, despite being late, Jim seemed like a nice guy. Plus, he was wickedly handsome.

This may turn out to be a fun night after all.

The hostess led them to a table on the outdoor terrace, where Jim pulled out Ellen's chair and helped her slide it in after she was seated. As he placed his suit jacket on the back of his chair, Ellen caught a glimpse of its lining. Silk. Impressive. He sat down and picked up the drinks menu.

"I'm so relieved that the work week is behind me," Jim said, his eyes transfixed on the list of beverage options. "You don't seem like a beer drinker to me. Interested in another cocktail or a glass of wine?" He placed the menu on the table. "I'm going to have a glass of the Girard Cabernet Sauvignon myself."

"Make that two," Ellen replied, delighted. "I like your choice. I actually visited Girard Winery when I flew out to Napa Valley with some girlfriends. It's beautiful there. Their wines are some of my favorites."

"Well, what do you know? We already have something in common—our superb taste in wines," Jim said affably. He winked.

Ellen laughed. She knew she was a bit buzzed from the mojito. Still, it seemed like he was flirting with her. *I'm good with that.*

Jim ordered their drinks, and after the server departed, he turned to her. "I hope you don't mind that I took the liberty of ordering for you too. It's just kind of my way."

"No problem," she responded honestly. She had all the sensibilities of an independent, self-sufficient woman. She owned her condominium, paid her bills on time, and was handier around the house than many of the men she dated. Yet Ellen wanted her future life partner to be a gentleman; a man whose considerate, even doting, acts would prove that chivalry was not dead, as so many of her female friends had come to believe. She had spent her life observing the genteel way her father treated her mother and wanted that dynamic to be present in the long-term relationship she hoped to be in one day.

The waiter returned with a half-full bottle of the Girard. He poured a splash of wine into Jim's glass. Ellen watched attentively as Jim swirled, sniffed, and tasted it. He seemed well-schooled at the art of wine tasting.

"The wine is most acceptable," Jim said to the waiter, who proceeded to dispense what remained in the bottle into their two awaiting glasses.

Drinks in hand, Ellen and Jim toasted to first dates. "This wine is always satisfying," Jim said as he leaned back in his chair and took a sip. "Bart Collins told me he's a good friend of your parents. He's set me up once before. That date was a complete bust. But I'm getting a different sense about this one. You're hot. You've got a great smile, and I already know you have excellent taste in wine. But before we proceed any further, I have a question to ask you."

While Ellen was delighted by the flattery, Jim's folded arms and his suddenly serious tone had her concerned.

"Sure, what is it?" she responded in as nonchalant a manner as she could muster.

"All week long I have to act proper and professionally at work. Bart and my other clients know me as a guy who is polite, responsive, and respectful. I give them sound advice and solve their legal problems. That's a big part of who I am. Here's the thing—I grew up in a household with a mother and father who swore like a pair of sailors. I realize that might seem atypical."

Ellen nodded as her concern mounted.

"Of course, I can't speak that way at work. So it gets all pent up. On the weekend I like to be the real me. What I want to know is, do you mind if I swear?"

Ellen waited a few moments before answering. *If I say no, he'll think I'm a prude. If I say yes, he'll unleash the real Jim, who likely isn't the classy gentleman that I'm thinking he is. But it's bet-ter if I let him be authentic.*

"Okay, you can swear if you'd like," she said hesitantly.

"Fuck, that's great. Thanks for being all right with it," Jim said. "Damn, I knew you would be cool about this. Bart has no idea about this side of me. Let's keep it that way, okay?"

Ellen nodded again but was speechless. It was the first time any of her dates had asked permission to swear.

Jim opened his dinner menu, smiling now that he could cuss freely. "Let's figure out what we're going to eat."

He proceeded to intersperse his commentary on the restau-rant's starter and entrée options with a steady barrage of f-bombs. Ellen looked at him quizzically.

He looks Ivy League–educated, but he's talking like he just climbed out of the gutter. What a peculiar guy! This evening is turning out to be more interesting than staying home and watching reruns of Modern Family.

Ellen chuckled at that thought.

"Hey, what's so funny?" Jim asked, peering around his menu.

"Oh, nothing. Really," Ellen responded. She didn't care to disclose what she'd been thinking.

Jim laughed. "You're such a bitch."

She abruptly put her menu down. "Excuse me. I'm a what?"

"You heard me. You're a bitch. But that's okay because I like bitches." Jim winked and went back to reading his menu.

Ellen stared at him, slack-jawed. *What just happened?* Yes, she'd said he could swear, but not at her! Jim had gone from bizarre to ridiculous. Did he think that calling her a bitch would turn her on? Even if he was only teasing, how dare he call her something so offensive! This guy didn't seem to understand women at all.

I'm done. Time to leave.

Ellen reached down to grab her purse from where it lay below her chair. Then she paused. How would she explain the date's early demise to Mr. Collins? She didn't want to insult him by telling him that the man he set her up with was a closeted profanity addict. He probably wouldn't believe her anyway. Ugh! Somehow, she needed to see this evening through.

Ellen sat back up and took shelter behind her menu. She inhaled deeply and exhaled slowly, just as she had learned to do in yoga class. The only way to endure this date was to become "Teflon Woman" and let his rude comments ricochet off her. She'd be pleasant and let him do most of the talking, something he obviously liked to do. But she knew one thing for sure: the flirting was over.

The waiter returned to take their dinner orders. They agreed to get the cherrystone clams and calamari for appetizers. For their main courses, Ellen chose the grilled salmon and Jim opted for the herb-crusted Atlantic halibut.

With the meal ordered, Jim and Ellen delved into many of the get-to-know-you topics that are often covered on a first date. She was born and raised in western Massachusetts. He grew up in Gloucester, on Cape Ann. They both had younger sisters. They both played sports during high school. Jim spent his college years at the University of Colorado at Boulder. Ellen went to UMass Amherst. Both had been in committed relationships, but neither had made it down the aisle. Travel was a passion they shared.

"Have you traveled much around the US?" Jim asked as he

took a bite of one of the clams that had just been served. "Not for business, but for pleasure."

"Yes, I have," Ellen responded. She quickly calculated the number of states she'd visited. "I've been to at least thirty-five states. It's the Deep South that I still need to explore, places like Mississippi, Alabama, and Arkansas. How about you?"

"Shit, I've passed through a lot of cities in the US, but not as a tourist," Jim replied. "Before I started my private practice, I had to fly all over the country visiting all these goddamn corporate clients, plus I needed to be at our Seattle office a few times a month. I got so fuckin' tired of all the flying that eight years ago I bought a ranch in Colorado."

This guy is full of surprises! He wears Brooks Brothers and owns a ranch out West. At least Mr. Collins was right about him being interesting.

"I've got a two-thousand-square-foot home on six acres of mostly wooded land. I loved the area during my college years, and I figured that having a place not too far from the Denver airport would cut my travel time, since I wouldn't always have to fly all the fuckin' way back to Boston."

"How's that worked out for you?" Ellen asked as she finished off the last calamari.

"It worked out really well when I was traveling almost weekly. But now that I'm not on the road as much, I don't get out to the ranch as often." Jim placed his fork down and leaned forward as though he was about to tell Ellen a secret. She remained sitting upright.

"There's something so fuckin' mesmerizing and humbling about the night sky in the Rockies. When I'm at the ranch, I often sleep outside. No tent. No sleeping pad. It's just me and my sleeping bag on the ground. Lying there, I stare up at the sky for hours, taking it all in. It's stunning. I've gotten very good at identifying the stars and planets. Are you into astronomy at all?"

"Somewhat. I used to love Carl Sagan's TV show *Cosmos*," Ellen said, "but that was years ago. Honestly, when I'm out at night in the city, it doesn't occur to me to look up at the sky. Instead, if I'm walking alone, I'm focused on staying alert to what's going on around me. Even if I did look up more often, it's probably impossible to see as dark a night sky. Not like what you see in Colorado."

"You're goddamn right about that," said Jim as their entrées were being placed on the table. Jim waited for Ellen to take her first bite before continuing. "One thing I haven't told you yet is that I'm a classical pianist. Piano has been part of my life since I was in grade school. The lessons started when I was nine, and I've been playing ever since."

"I'm impressed," Ellen said. "I don't know many—make that *any*—classically trained pianists. Do you play regularly?"

"Definitely. I have a grand piano in my condo. If I've had a rough day, I'll come home and play for hours. Playing helps me work through whatever bullshit I've been dealing with at the office." Jim took another bite of the halibut.

"My view of the Harbor Islands is fuckin' remarkable. There I am. I'll be sitting at the piano, playing into the night. Looking out the window at the bay, I'll sometimes feel longings for the open sky and the quiet of the Rockies. So occasionally, I'll walk down to Waterfront Park, climb into the bushes, and sleep there.

The sounds of boats bobbing at the marina and the water brushing up against the docks are very calming. And there's the night sky over the harbor to take in. I sleep well."

Ellen halted mid-bite. "Seriously? You sleep in the bushes as though you're homeless?"

"Yes, I sleep in the bushes. But not like some fuckin' homeless person, because I'm not homeless." Ellen sensed a mix of exasperation and pride from Jim. "I'm drawn to the outdoors and being surrounded by nature overnight. It's urban camping. At least that's how I think of it."

Jim paused and looked across the dining hall. "I'm going to use the restroom. I'll be back."

Ellen sat back in her chair as soon as he stepped away, feeling like she'd returned to the realm of the bizarre. It was surreal. If the guy weren't sitting across from her, she wouldn't believe that a person like him existed! Thankfully, he didn't seem dangerous. Still, she was ready for the date to be over.

I'm saying no to dessert.

"That was a nicely decorated men's room," Jim remarked upon his return. "I really liked the grass-cloth wallpaper. Maybe I'll use something similar in the bathroom at my place. I'm redecorating." As he was sitting down, he asked, "Do you want to order some dessert?"

"Thanks, but no. The salmon was surprisingly filling." Ellen was grateful for convenient truths.

"Shit, I'm not much of a dessert person myself," Jim said. "Hey, while I was in the head, I was thinking . . . In two weeks, I'll be going to the ranch for the Fourth of July weekend. How about you come with me?"

Ellen's eyes opened wider. "Wow, that's very nice of you," she said, knowing she needed to come up with a credible excuse, fast. She couldn't possibly fly to Colorado with someone she'd just met, especially someone as rude as Jim! "But a friend from Chicago is staying with me that weekend. We went to high school together and haven't seen each other for a few years. So thanks, but I won't be able to go."

The excuse was nicely done. Or so she thought, until he started gazing at her with an annoying Cheshire Cat grin.

"What? Why are you looking at me like that?" she asked.

"You're such a dick," he said, laughing casually.

Ellen gripped the stem of her wine glass. "That's really offensive! I'm not a dick. Why would you say such a thing?"

It didn't matter how he responded. She refused to engage in whatever manipulative game he wanted to play.

Calm down. Let his words ricochet off me. Remember, I'm Teflon Woman. Ellen relaxed her grip.

"I don't know. I wanted to get you riled up, I suppose. You're sexy when you're riled up. Did you know that?" Jim asked. "I wouldn't have called you a dick if you'd said yes to coming to Colorado with me."

"Would you like any dessert, coffee, or tea?" the server interrupted. Consumed by their conversation, Ellen had been unaware of the waiter's presence.

"Nope, I'm good," Ellen responded immediately.

"I'm good too," Jim echoed.

"All right then, enjoy the rest of your evening, and thanks for dining with us." The waiter placed the check folder on the table.

"I've got it," Jim said. He removed his wallet from his back pants pocket, deposited a credit card on the folder, and handed both items back to the waiter without bothering to look at the bill.

"Thanks for dinner. The food was good," Ellen said.

"You're welcome. It's been a good time too," Jim replied, placing his brown cowhide wallet on the table.

It was nice of him to pay, especially since I'm never going out on a date with him again. But how is it possible that he thinks tonight is going well?

"What plans do you have for the weekend?" she asked to fill the time until the waiter returned.

"Piano. I plan on playing a lot of piano. I'll probably get at least an hour's playing time in before bed. Then tomorrow night, I'll be at Symphony Hall. The Boston Symphony Orchestra is performing Rachmaninoff's Third Piano Concerto. It's a fuckin' incredibly complex and challenging piece that requires immense stamina and endurance to get through and play well. I've attempted it before, but my rendition is crap."

While Jim signed the bill that had been returned to the table, Ellen picked up her purse, pulled out her black wool pashmina, and wrapped it around her shoulders. The breeze off the harbor had taken on a slight chill.

"Thanks for dinner," she repeated.

Jim stood and took a few steps toward her. Choosing not to wait for him to attend to her chair, she slid it back decisively, rose, and started for the exit. Jim quickly put on his jacket and followed. As Ellen walked ahead, she heard him call out, "Nice ass!" She rolled her eyes and accelerated her pace. She walked out the restaurant's front door and stopped on the sidewalk.

"How did you get to the restaurant? Did you drive?" Jim asked after catching up with her.

"Yes, I did. But there's no need for you to walk me to my car. It's not too far away, just around the corner," Ellen said, pointing to her right. "Plus, there's a taxi right there for you. Taxi!" she yelled, vigorously waving her hand in the air. The taxi stopped along the curb.

"You're good!" Jim remarked. Taking a step toward Ellen, he wrapped his arms around her in a light embrace. "All right, I'll talk to you soon."

Ellen nodded slightly and watched as Jim stepped into the taxi. It pulled away and she let out a long sigh.

"Damn, that was an insane date!" Ellen said before turning around and heading for her car.

The Rest of the Story

When Ellen got home, she plugged her cell phone into the charger and turned the phone off. The next morning there was a voice mail from Jim telling her that he'd had a very nice time and that he'd been thinking about her—*and* her ass—as he'd been playing his piano for the last two hours. The message was time-stamped 2:30 a.m.

Ellen never called him back. Nor did she give Mr. or Mrs. Collins the details of the date. Instead, she opted to tell them that she didn't feel a connection with Jim. A few weeks later, her mother relayed that Mrs. Collins had made a comment about Ellen's dating standards being too high. When Ellen disclosed all that had happened that night, her mom was horrified. But in the end, they decided not to share the details with either Mr. or Mrs. Collins.

Dating Takeaway Tips

STAND UP FOR YOURSELF.

If you're on a date with a difficult person, don't be passive and let them hurt your feelings, ramrod your opinions, or treat you badly. Tell them that you object to what they have said or done. You can say, "I'm sure you mean well, but I want you to know that I feel uncomfortable (or annoyed, disturbed, or whatever else you're feeling) with what you've just said (or done)." Make sure to say it in as calm and controlled a manner as possible. Don't lower yourself to their level. Don't raise your voice. If they are an argumentative person, or someone who's inclined toward violence, you don't want to escalate their reaction to your response to the point that they'd be physically abusive. Most importantly, you want to behave in a way that retains your dignity and self-respect. If you feel that it's not worth the agony of possibly facing more aggression, then gracefully excuse yourself and leave.

DON'T TAKE IT PERSONALLY.

If your date says critical or negative things about you, don't take it personally. Build a Teflon shield around you, just as Ellen did. Don't put any value on his words. Let them bounce off you. Don't care about what he thinks. He's the problem, not you.

DO MORE LISTENING THAN TALKING.

You know about you. You're there to learn about your date. Be an active listener and ask questions from a place of genuine curiosity. Hear what your date is saying and infer what they're not. Listen for how they treat people, the choices they've made, and what they regard as right and wrong. These kernels of information are pieces of the large puzzle that you're trying to put together to answer an important question: Do you want to get to know this person better?

IF YOU DON'T FEEL SAFE, END THE DATE EARLY.

There are all sorts of ways to get out of a date quickly. The classic approach is to go to the bathroom and call or text a friend or family member. Ask them to phone you in a few minutes with a fake crisis. When the call comes in, say that an emergency has happened and that you must leave. No date is worth risking your physical or mental well-being over.

"I have known great men and not so great men.
But the trenches of dating have taught me what I want
and don't want. Who I am and who I want to be."

— *Jennifer Love Hewitt*
actress and author

An Evening in the Desert

C lark stood in Raven's front doorway with a bouquet of orange and pink roses in his outstretched hand. Never before
had a man brought flowers when he'd come to pick her up for a
first date. The gesture was especially unexpected since just a few
hours earlier Clark and Raven had moved their blind date up
one day earlier, to that evening.

Raven had listened to an unexpected voice mail from her
friend Michelle three weeks earlier. "There's a guy at work. His
name is Kevin. He was telling me that his brother, Clark, is going through a rough divorce. His wife cheated on him! Can you
believe it? So, I've never met Clark, but since Kevin is a nice guy,
I figure that his brother probably will be too. I hope you won't
be mad at me, but I gave Kevin your number to give to Clark. I
know it's a long shot that things will work, but I figured, why
not? Call me."

Raven was anything but mad. The possibility of this setup
came at an auspicious time. After living in Phoenix for twenty
years, she had begun to tire of the city's singles scene. Raven and
her girlfriends had been spotting too many familiar male faces
out at the bars on Friday and Saturday nights.

45

"Instead of getting dressed up and going out to flirt with a recycled pool of men, I'm going to stay home more on the weekends," she'd told her roommate, Valerie, over coffee one morning. "The long days at work are exhausting me. I haven't watched *Saturday Night Live*, or any late-night TV, in ages. I could use some laughs, and those shows are a lot funnier than the guys I've been meeting lately."

Clark called two weeks later.

"Hi! How are you?" Raven asked after he introduced himself.

"I'm terrified," said the voice on the other end of the line.

"No need to be," she said. Raven quietly cleared her throat and then asked about his brother, Kevin. He was the only person in Clark's life that she knew of.

"He's the reason I moved to Arizona. I stayed in St. Petersburg after I graduated from Eckerd College. When I was in school, the town was fun. But it got old pretty fast afterward."

"I know what you mean," Raven interjected. "Arizona State University is in Tempe, but I commuted from Phoenix. So I've essentially been living in my college town for two decades. At this point, I know it too well."

"You get it," Clark said. "I was feeling done with Florida. Kevin had moved here, so I followed him. That was five years ago. Then I got married. But that's a story for another time."

From there, the conversation wound around topics. They discussed their families, their jobs, where they each grew up, their favorite restaurants, their shared love of music, and their spiritual beliefs. They eventually agreed that they should meet in person.

"Edie Brickell is performing in Tempe on Sunday night. My roommate, her fiancé, and I are planning on going. How about you join us?" Raven asked.

"That sounds cool. Her band was one of my favorites years back," Clark said. They arranged where to meet. She'd text him to let him know what she was wearing. Raven hung up and immediately called Michelle.

"Clark seems great. He's coming to the concert on Sunday night!"

"I'm so happy!" Michelle responded. "I had a hunch that the two of you should meet."

The workweek that followed was a demanding one for Raven. It was her excitement about meeting Clark on Sunday night that fueled her through an onslaught of meetings and multiple project deadlines.

Saturday morning her cell phone rang. "Hi, Raven, this is Clark. I know we have plans for tomorrow night, but colleagues of mine are going to see a punk rock festival tonight. I was thinking that it would be fun for you and me to join them. Are you up for it? Or do you have other plans?"

"Sure, I'm up for it," Raven replied reflexively.

"Awesome! The show's about a thirty-minute drive from downtown Phoenix. How about I pick you up?" Clark asked.

Raven hesitated.

His offer was gentlemanly, but she'd never had a blind date pick her up before. *Do I really want to break my dating rules?* Valerie was away that night, so no one would see him or make sure she got home okay. *Take the risk, Raven.* She wanted to listen to her gut, even though she was sure her mom would tell her not to.

"All right, you can, but I'm okay with meeting you there too. Coming to get me from Mesa is going to add a lot more time to your drive."

"Nope, it's not a problem at all. I'll come get you," he said.

After they hung up, Raven took some safety precautions. She called Michelle and Valerie and let them know her plans. It was agreed that if they didn't hear from her by 11:30 p.m., they would call or text her to make sure everything was fine.

Raven's heart was racing as she opened the front door that evening. Before her stood a man with dusty brown hair, wire-rimmed glasses, and brown eyes. The bouquet of vibrant roses he was holding complemented the bright fluorescent orange T-shirt tucked into his Levi's.

Wow, he's cute! He's better looking than I'd expected.

"They're from my garden," Clark said. "Believe it or not, I have ten rose bushes on my property."

"Thanks so much," Raven replied. A big smile blossomed on her face as she accepted his gift. "They are stunning! Give me a moment."

Raven left Clark standing at the front door as she raced to the kitchen. She poured water into an empty vase, put the flowers into it, and placed the roses on the kitchen table.

Raven grabbed her sweater and purse off the couch on the way back to the foyer. "I'm ready to go if you are."

"Absolutely, let's get going," Clark said. "A light sweater is probably not a bad idea for an April evening in the desert."

Raven locked the door and they headed to his truck. He darted ahead of her as they approached the vehicle and opened the passenger-side door. Raven got in and quickly scanned the interior. There was no gun rack, no bags of chewing tobacco, and no packs of cigarettes in sight—all good signs by her account. The cab's pristine condition told her that either he was a very clean guy or he wanted her to think he was.

Never comfortable with extended silences, Raven did most of the talking during their drive through the city and desert. After Clark asked whether she was glad she went to ASU, she delved into what it was like being the only woman in the School of Technology's engineering program.

"Well, for better or worse, the professors usually learned my name right away," she said. "They probably noticed when I wasn't in class too. It's hard to blend in when you're the only person in the room with breasts and wavy brown hair like Jennifer Beals in *Flashdance*." He laughed. Raven liked the sound of it.

"'You do look a lot like her. I know it was a chick flick, but I loved that movie," Clark said, diverting his eyes from the road to smile and wink at Raven.

She grinned, her cheeks feeling warm, and looked out the window. A towering saguaro cactus stood just a few yards from the freeway. Light green and brown desert grasses melded together as they drove, and every now and then a cactus whizzed by. Raven loved the flat, bleak landscape.

"The desert has such a sense of mystery to it, don't you think?" she asked. "On the topic of mysteries, who are these friends of yours that we're meeting at the show?"

"Barry is a friend from work. He's a graphic designer like I am. We work in the same group. He's bringing his girlfriend, Brenda. Then there are two other guys from the marketing department, Michael and Bill, and their girlfriends, who I don't know." Clark took his eyes off the road for a moment and looked at Raven. "I think you'll like my friends. Both Brenda and you have good senses of humor."

The venue was not far off the highway. Clark easily found a parking space at the end of a long row of vehicles packed with pickup trucks and SUVs. They got out of his truck, stepped onto the disintegrating asphalt pavement, and walked across the parking lot to the stadium.

They breezed through the security checkpoint. Clark presented the tickets to the usher and causally remarked to Raven, "We've got lawn seats, which actually means that we don't have seats at all. But we do get to pick our own plot to watch the show from."

After stopping to buy two beers, two hot dogs, and a large bag of chips, all paid for by Clark, they proceeded onto a poorly maintained grass field. Flanking the stage were two tall towers of black speakers playing background music from the '80s. The entire area in front of it was packed at least fifteen yards deep with people, both seated and standing. The field behind the crowd was dotted with smaller satellites of concertgoers. A gentle breeze wafted the scents of popcorn and steaming hot dogs from the concessions area across the field.

Clark followed Raven as she crossed the lawn. "How about we sit here?" she asked, pointing toward a patch of green grass. There was a direct line of sight to the stage, but it was removed enough from the crowd and the huge black speakers that they wouldn't have to scream over deafening music to talk.

"Works for me," Clark said. His phone rang not long after

they sat down. Raven overheard Clark's end of the conversation: "Oh no . . . that sucks. Will they be coming soon?" He paused, frowning as the other person replied. "Let me know how things turn out. See you, man."

Clark hung up.

"What happened?" Raven asked. She'd already deduced that his friends were running late.

"Barry's car has a flat tire and there's no spare," Clark said. "They're stuck on the highway. They have to wait for a tow truck to take them back to a garage in Phoenix that may, or may not, have a replacement tire. Chances are that a mechanic isn't going to be there so late to patch the tire either. That sucks for them."

A smile appeared on Clark's face. "On the other hand, I guess that means it's just you and me tonight. Are you okay with that?"

"I am," Raven replied, returning his smile with a sizable one of her own.

The concert started soon after. The punk rock music that blared across the ballpark was background noise for Raven and Clark. They spent the entire show talking, laughing, eating, and drinking. As the evening passed, they unconsciously moved closer to each other until they sat just inches apart.

Clark was busy telling Raven about a prank he and his brother pulled on their dad during a family vacation years earlier when the last note of the encore song was played and the lead singer yelled out, "Good night, Phoenix!" The concertgoers who had filled in the vacant parcels of grass around them during the show were up on their feet clapping. Realizing that they were the only people sitting out the standing ovation, Raven and Clark bolted up and applauded vigorously. Raven glanced over at Clark as he clapped.

He's such a nice man.

As if on cue, Clark turned to her, leaned over, and gently kissed her. Raven instinctively closed her eyes and took in the exquisite sensation of his lips on hers. They were soft, warm, familiar. No words were said as he lifted his head and turned back toward the stage. Raven savored the moment and then enthusiastically joined in with the chorus of fans cheering around them. As she did, Clark placed his right arm around her shoulder. A rush of warmth flooded through Raven's body, culminating in a glowing smile. She looked over at Clark and then turned her attention to the stage.

The music stopped. The lights were switched on. Raven started to put her black sweater on over her fuchsia blouse.

"Well, it's time to get going," she said.

"Yeah, I guess you're right," Clark said, looking down at the remains of their meal on the ground below them.

Raven gathered up the food wrappers and the bottles and placed them in the empty chip bag.

"Here, let me take care of that," Clark said. He took the trash from Raven's hands and walked it to the closest garbage can.

When they got back to his truck, Clark again opened the passenger-side door for Raven before getting in and starting the engine.

"That was a great show," she said.

"Are you sure? We really didn't watch much of it, did we?" he asked with a chuckle. The line of cars exiting the parking lot was gradually moving forward. "That was a killer finale, but the rest of it, I'm not so sure about. What I am sure about is that you're an interesting woman and fun to talk to."

"Why, thanks! You're fun to talk to as well. How about I find a station with good reception out here for us to listen to?" she asked. Raven reached for the radio's dials.

"What in the world?" Clark declared, looking at his dashboard's dials quizzically. "I'm almost out of gas!" He was silent for a moment, seemingly thinking about what to do next. "I hope you don't mind if I take a detour and stop at a gas station first?"

Raven's concerns about driving so far out of town alone with a guy she barely knew suddenly resurfaced.

Oh, great. First his supposed friends no-show us. Then suddenly we're making an unexpected detour. I'm bones in the desert! He's going to do me in and leave me to rot! Do I jump out and run for it now?

"Uh, okay," she replied tentatively.

Raven held her breath the entire ride. She tried to distract herself from wondering if he was really taking her to a gas station, or if he had concocted a ruse, by switching between radio stations.

"You can't find one that you like?" Clark asked after she'd sampled at least eight of them.

"No, I can't seem to," she said a bit curtly.

"Okay, but when it comes to music, I'm easy to please. I'm into rock, punk, pop, eighties, and country music, so most of those stations that you just whizzed by would be fine with me."

Raven kept moving the dial from station to station.

"Here's the exit I want to take," Clark said a few minutes later. They pulled off the road and into a Shell station. Clark got out of the truck and pumped the gas as Raven used her side-view mirror to monitor his every move.

As Clark approached the car after he'd finished, Raven removed her hand from the door handle that she'd been unconsciously gripping. She noticed that moisture remained on the metal where her palm had previously been.

Clark stepped back into the driver's seat. "Sorry about that," he said. "I usually pay attention to how much fuel is in the tank. But it completely slipped my mind that I'd probably need to get more gas. I was so focused on making tonight right for you." He started the engine and pulled out toward the road.

Thank goodness! I'm going to live! This guy is trustworthy after all.

"No problem," Raven replied, flattered by the compliment he'd paid her. "It happens to the best of us. I appreciate all that you've done to put our date together."

"You got it," he said, smiling broadly. "It's not every day that a guy gets to spend time with a beautiful woman like you!"

"Right back at you," she said, playfully brushing her hand against his right shoulder.

Raven glanced at the clock on the truck's dashboard. It was 11:20 p.m.

"I hope you don't mind, but I just remembered I have to text someone," she said.

She reached into her purse and pulled out her phone. The text to her two friends read: "*Clark is awesome! Heading home now. More details tomorrow.*"

The drive back to Phoenix flew by as the Eurythmics' "Sweet Dreams" and INXS's "Need You Tonight" played on the classic '80s radio station Raven had finally selected. They both sang along to some of the retro tunes.

Clark parked the truck in a spot right in front of her apartment building. "Can I walk you to your door?" he asked.

"Yes, you may," she replied.

"Are we still on for the concert tomorrow night?" Clark asked as they strolled up the path.

"We are. It will be fun to see another show with you," Raven said. "Why don't you come over at six and we can all drive together?"

"That's an excellent idea," Clark said. They reached her front door. He leaned over and gently kissed her. Raven kept her eyes closed after their lips had parted to soak in the tingly warm feeling flowing through her body. When she opened them, she saw Clark smiling at her.

"You know, it's been four years since I was on a date with someone new," he said. "I wasn't sure how tonight would go, but it's been great."

"Yes, it has," Raven said. "And I have a feeling that tomorrow will be too!"

"I'll see you then," Clark said.

Raven opened her door, stepped into her apartment, and turned around to watch Clark get back into his truck. She waved and smiled as he drove away.

Until tomorrow night!

The Rest of the Story

Raven and Clark enjoyed a whirlwind romance. Their decision to date exclusively was made just a few weeks after the Edie Brickell concert. Clark's divorce was finalized two months into their relationship. He proposed to Raven in October, a mere seven months after their blind date. Raven and Clark got married two years later.

Dating Takeaway Tips

GO ON BLIND DATES.

If someone you know and trust wants to set you up, accept their offer, unless you have a very compelling reason why you shouldn't (for example, the guy is an ex-boyfriend). People's lives are so busy these days that when someone takes the time to try to bring two people together, it's a tribute to their kindness to say yes. Be open to the recommendation but try not to judge the match that was made. Even if the person you're introduced to isn't up to your "standards," be gracious with your friend and don't make it mean anything (such as, "Wow—that's what my friend thinks of me?"). Remember, your friends and family are doing their best and just want to see you happy. Their recommendation has no bearing on what they think of you.

BE FLEXIBLE.

If the plans change, roll with it, as long as your safety is not at risk. Things could turn out better than you expected.

BE OPEN-MINDED.

Don't be judgmental. It takes a while to get to know someone. Chemistry and attraction build over time. Relax and ask casual questions to get to know your date. If you are completely turned off by them, figure out if there's anything interesting you can learn from your conversation. Maybe they've traveled somewhere you want to go or have eaten at a restaurant you want to try and can recommend the best dishes to order.

TAKE SAFETY PRECAUTIONS.

When you're spending time with someone you don't know, always tell friends or family members where you are going to be and when. Create a check-in plan with them. Follow through with it. If you're uncomfortable doing what your date suggests, such as going to their home, getting in their car, being physical, meeting them somewhere you don't want to be, or giving out your contact information, then don't. Propose another meeting place or activity. Tell them that it's easier for you to continue messaging through the app and communicate that way until you feel more at ease. Pleasing *them* isn't what you should be focused on. Instead, continually check in with *yourself* to determine what feels safe to you. As the saying goes, "Better safe than sorry." Your safety should always come first.

"Don't look for a partner who is eye candy.
Look for a partner who is soul food."

— *Karen Salmansohn*

Founder, NotSalmon.com

How'd You Like to Treat Me?

K eisha and Rob had decided to meet in the lobby of the St. Francis Hotel. The Union Square landmark was convenient to both their workplaces and to the bar where they'd be going for a drink.

Keisha arrived first. She had left her trade show shift early so she could get off her feet and relax for a few minutes before the date started. When she passed through the hotel's revolving door, she made a beeline to the empty couch she spotted in the hotel lobby, dropped her purse and laptop bag, and sunk into the overstuffed velvet red cushions. Keisha closed her eyes and tried to block out the noise from tourists chatting nearby and the passing police sirens seeping in from the street.

Keisha and Rob's auspicious meeting had happened at a friend's holiday party three weeks earlier. The buffet line had been moving at a snail's pace. As Keisha inched her way forward, her stomach rumbled. Then it rumbled again. She continued talking to the woman behind her in line, hoping it had gone unnoticed. When there were only two people between her and the stack of plates and silverware, a man suddenly stepped in front of her.

She stared at his back, her face getting red. Her muscles

tightened. Then he turned around and smiled at her, a warm smile with a tinge of mischievousness. Intrigue washed her anger away. Keisha smiled back.

"You know, cutting in line at a Christmas party isn't a holiday-spirited thing to do," she said with a lilt in her voice.

"I know. I'm really sorry, but I'm famished," he replied, balancing his plate while extending his hand. "I'm Rob."

He's cute, she thought as she shook his hand. *He reminds me of Greg Kinnear but with darker brown hair.*

They chatted their way through the buffet line, throughout the meal, and over post-dessert drinks. He was a lawyer who had taken refuge in California from the Manhattan legal life. She was a sales account manager at a consumer goods company. They both had spent years putting their jobs first and their personal lives second. They were in their early forties. She was divorced. He hadn't been married and refused to date online. She was fine with dating apps. He had some funny stories to share, and she liked his sense of humor.

They exchanged e-mails and phone numbers. He texted her the next day. Would she like to meet him for a drink? Her text was brief: "*Yes!*"

A few more texts back and forth, and their plans were set.

When Rob walked through the revolving front door of the St. Francis Hotel, he spotted Keisha immediately. He was wearing a dark brown blazer that reminded her of one her dad owned. He had paired it with jeans and looked retro-hip.

They exchanged a friendly but somewhat awkward A-frame hug. Keisha noticed that he stood eye to eye with her. That put him at five foot ten.

"Are you ready to get a drink?" he asked.

"Absolutely. I've never been to a speakeasy before. This will be fun," Keisha said. She picked up her bags and they headed out.

There'd been a bar in the building they were walking to since 1867. During the Prohibition era, it was transformed into an illegal speakeasy, and then was turned back into a legal bar after the passage of the 21st Amendment. New owners had recently restored the place into a modernized version of its 1920s self. There had been a lot of local buzz about it, even though the neighborhood had become rather sketchy, with drug deals happening all too often in plain sight.

When Keisha and Rob arrived at Bourbon & Branch's numberless door, Rob pressed the bell. The door opened slightly. Keisha heard a female voice ask, "What's the password?"

"Quiff," Rob answered through the doorjamb.

The door to the windowless building opened fully, and they stepped into the dimly lit lounge.

The club was small, but the interior decor was striking. A long wooden bar ran the length of the right side of the room. On the brick wall behind it hung two glass shelves lined with bottles of hard alcohol, and above the shelves a chalkboard listed the day's special cocktails. Along the left side of the lounge were table lamp–lit booths. From the copper ceiling hung a stunning four-tiered glass chandelier with glass spears jettisoning out of it.

The hostess escorted Rob and Keisha to a booth toward the rear of the lounge. While they were sliding across the leather-upholstered benches, she placed two menus on the antique oak table and departed.

The speakeasy's menu was an encyclopedia of spirits and cocktails. The selection of cocktails boasted colorful and varied names—White Lady, Negroni, Dempsey, Lonsdale, Harvest Manhattan, Cracked Thumb, The Sceptre. Keisha noticed that there was no food, not even a bowl of nuts, on it. She had worked a daylong shift at the trade show. Lunch had been an energy bar. Surveying the menu, she realized she should have eaten more to lessen the potency of the drink she'd be consuming.

Oh, well. There's nothing I can do about it now.

A thin, heavily tattooed brunette approached.

"How are the two of you doing tonight?" she asked enthusiastically. "My name is Terry. Have either of you been here before?"

After Rob and Keisha responded that they hadn't, Terry shifted into tour guide mode. She walked them through the menu. They peppered her with questions about the hard alcohol and mixed drinks they hadn't encountered before.

Keisha chose the Cubakula, a special seasonal cocktail. Its main ingredient was rum, her favorite liquor. Rob selected the more traditional Pimm's Cup. With their libation decisions made, Terry collected the menus and headed over to the bar to place the order.

"So, Rob, what do you like to do for fun?" Keisha asked, volleying the first personal question of the evening.

"My profession is law, but my passion is improvisation," Rob said. "Every week I take a class at BATS School of Improv. I'm hoping to eventually become one of their main-stage company players."

"Wow, you're really serious about it!" Keisha said. "What do you like about doing improv?"

"The main reason I like improv is because it unlocks potential in a sea of uncertainty," Rob said. "I don't know where a scene is going–and furthermore, it's not up to me. Ideally, it's a process explored by everyone who is participating in it. Sometimes scenes that look like they're going nowhere turn into something magical." Rob picked up his water glass and drank until almost half was gone.

"Talking about improv must make me thirsty," he said after placing the glass back on the table.

"Don't worry. I'm sure our real drinks will be here soon," Keisha said. She winked and he laughed.

"About your question, I like how doing improv offers lots of lessons for everyday life. I try to have more scenes that work better than ones that don't, and I try to forgive myself if they bomb. I often want a scene to go one way; it sometimes turns out another. I can resist or I can accept. In improv, resisting only makes the scene worse. I have a suspicion that the same is true in life." He looked away for a moment and then back at Keisha, his eyes glowing with enthusiasm. "Hey, how about I take you through one of my recent improvs? I know there's not a lot of space here, but I'll give it a try if you'd like."

So much for casual chitchat. What's going to happen here?

"Sure, go ahead," Keisha said, a little apprehensive.

Just then the drinks were served. After the waitress stepped away, they raised their glasses.

"Here's to unlocking potential," Rob said. The glasses clinked and they took their first sips.

Keisha coughed and shook her head slightly. "I wasn't expecting the Cubakula to be so strong."

Rob hurled back most of his Pimm's Cup, placed the glass back on the table, and launched into a scene he'd improvised in class. Watching Rob contend with the constraints of the booth while trying to portray a fireman responding to a blaze started by a heavily candled birthday cake, Keisha realized that her first date had devolved into a theater performance. She took another taste of her cocktail, and then another. Her giggles grew louder with every sip. She became numb to repeated glances directed their way by the couple seated across from them.

After putting out the birthday cake flames and saving the town from almost certain Armageddon, Rob reenacted the scene he'd done two weeks earlier about a guy who decides to spend all his lottery winnings on gourmet food for his cat. The waitress approached just as Rob was explaining how caught off guard he was when, mid-scene, his improv partner unexpectedly switched from the role of chef to undertaker.

"I've been hearing a lot of laughter coming from over here," Terry said. "You two sure like to have fun on Friday nights!"

"Actually, this is our first date," Keisha responded immediately.

Why did I clarify our status so quickly? He's entertaining, but do I really want to get serious with a guy who acts like this in public?

"Really? I wouldn't have thought that. Since it is, the two of you should know that I have a great track record with first dates. Many of the blind dates, setups, and online dates who've sat in my section have ended up in relationships," Terry boasted. "I kid you not. There was even one couple that got married!" Terry glanced at Keisha and then over at Rob.

"I've got a good feeling about the two of you. You seem to work. Speaking of work," she continued, "there are only thirty minutes left on your reservation. It's my job to get you another drink if you want one. Sorry. I probably should have come over earlier. Would you like something else?"

Rob looked at Keisha, whose glass was also empty. She nodded.

"I think we both can down another round in that amount of time," he said. "We'll have two of the same."

"Okay, coming right up," Terry said, and then headed off to an awaiting bartender.

"Can you believe that their reservations have time limits?" Rob threw his hands up. "Well, there's nothing we can do about it except enjoy the remaining minutes that we have here."

Why does he seem so surprised? He informed me about the reservation policy when we e-mailed to set up our date, Keisha wondered as she took a sip of her water.

"I realize I've been doing all of the talking," Rob said. "You talk for a while. Tell me more about you. What do you like to do for fun?"

Keisha told him about her love for travel. He felt the same. She shared with him the highlights of her trips to Indonesia and Venezuela. They were in the midst of a lengthy conversation about the best train rides they'd taken when Terry returned with their second round of drinks. Keisha was listening to Rob recount his visit to Brazil's Iguazu Falls when she realized her laugh had ratcheted up a few decibels. She looked around. The room was swaying slightly.

I must be buzzed. Dang!

She'd been afraid that would happen. The reservation had almost ended, but she couldn't drive home just yet. She knew she'd better eat something.

Keisha considered her options. She could say good night to Rob and grab some dinner or ask him to join her. She didn't like to dine alone. *Plus, he's funny and kind of cute.*

"Any interest in getting dinner afterward?" she asked. "I'd probably be breaking the law if I got behind the wheel right now. I need some food and some coffee. But if you have to get going, I understand."

Rob looked at his watch and then up at her. "Okay, sure. Where would you like to eat?"

Her mind was blurred by the effects of the alcohol. She didn't know the neighborhood well, and it was almost 9:30 p.m. Some restaurants would be closing soon. She was about to pick up her phone and do a search for restaurants nearby when it came to her. "How about Le Colonial? It's a little on the expensive side, but the food is good and it's not too far away. Just a few blocks back toward the St. Francis Hotel."

"Okay, if you recommend it, I'm in," Rob replied as Terry placed the check on the table. Both Keisha and Rob looked at the check folder for a few seconds until Rob tentatively reached for it.

Sensing some hesitation on his part to pay, Keisha said, "If you'd like me to, I can throw in some money."

I wonder if he picked up on my reluctance? It's our first date, after all. He should pay.

"No, the drinks are on me," Rob said. He placed his credit card on top of the bill and closed the folder. Smiling at Keisha, he leaned forward and touched her hand that was resting on the base of her empty glass. "As soon as the bill is taken care of, let's go get some dinner."

Once out of the bar, Keisha did her best to walk quickly. Her speed was fueled by her dual desires to eat and to get to a safer neighborhood. But she felt slightly off-balance. As they crossed the street, she noticed a pothole in front of her only seconds before she was about to plunge her foot straight into it. She leaped to the right to avoid the hole, landed a bit off-center, and grabbed Rob's arm to keep herself from falling.

"Whoa, you okay?" he asked, startled by her sudden move.

"Yes, I am, thanks," she replied, her cheeks instantly warming.

Am I embarrassed or am I buzzed? Or both?

He didn't try to pull his arm away, and she was glad to have the support. They walked the remaining three blocks arm in arm. Any passersby would have assumed they'd known one another for more than a few hours.

The host at Le Colonial sat them right away. Keisha was relieved. With the menu opened before her, she scanned the descriptions of all the dishes the French Vietnamese restaurant had to offer. Keisha decided to order the seared five-spice Peking duck breast that came with crispy Brussels sprouts.

No wine for me tonight. I need to sober up.

Rob was looking intently at his menu, seemingly reading every word. Keisha sat quietly surveying the restaurant. The main dining room had been designed to evoke the feel of 1920s French Vietnam. It seemed straight out of a scene from the movie *Indochine*. Dark brown rattan chairs surrounded white-clothed tables. Brown wooden fans, hung from the pressed tin ceiling, circled languorously overhead. Rectangular mirrors and louvered shutters were set into the white wainscoted walls, with vintage black-and-white photographs hung above them. Tropical plants adorned the corners of the room. The flooring alternated between green tile and patterned carpeting.

A tall, Scandinavian-looking man in a tuxedo soon appeared at their table, breaking the silence between them. "Good evening and welcome to Le Colonial. I'll be your server this evening. Are you ready to order?"

"We are. I'll have the Peking duck," Keisha said. "No starter or wine for me." Her entrée had a twenty-five-dollar price tag. She didn't want to run the tab up too high. It was a first date, after all.

The waiter turned to Rob. "How about you, sir?"

"I'll start with a glass of your house red," Rob said. "I'm a vegetarian. I'd like to have your beef with coconut curry dish, but without the beef. Can you ask the chef if he will substitute tofu for the beef but keep the rest of the dish as is? This is an Asian restaurant. You have tofu, right?"

"Ah, yes, we do serve tofu, although I'm not sure if the substitution can be made, sir," the waiter said. He tapped his notepad with his pen, seemingly thinking through Rob's request. "I'll be right back." He turned and walked toward the kitchen.

"How long have you been a vegetarian?" Keisha asked in an attempt to get the dinner conversation going.

"About eleven years," Rob replied. "After I read the chapter on chicken slaughtering in Michael Pollan's book *The Omnivore's Dilemma*, I was done eating two- and four-legged animals." Rob gently placed his hand on Keisha's shoulder. "But don't worry that you ordered duck. It doesn't bother me."

Keisha twitched her shoulder forward slightly to unseat his hand from where it rested. She didn't care what he thought of her meal choice.

The waiter soon returned. "Sir, I'm happy to inform you that the chef can accommodate your request."

"Terrific!" said Rob. "But here's the thing. I don't want to pay twenty-seven dollars for it. You've just agreed to remove expensive beef and replace it with inexpensive tofu. So I'll pay twenty dollars. Could you please go talk to the manager, or whomever you need to, and get him to agree to my price?" Rob sat back in his seat and crossed his arms.

The waiter stared at Rob, his eyebrows raised. Keisha couldn't believe her ears either. She stared at Rob, a mishmash of colliding thoughts racing through her head.

What in the world just happened? This guy is negotiating the cost of his meal as he would a used car!

As though he'd pressed an internal reset button, the waiter relaxed his eyebrows and straightened his bow tie. "I must say that this is very unorthodox, sir. Still, I will do as you asked and talk to the manager."

Keisha glared at Rob. "How could you do that? That was awful! So tactless! We're in a fine restaurant. We're not standing on the street corner buying tacos from a food truck!" Keisha said as soon as the waiter was out of earshot. She stopped and attempted to compose herself. The couple seated two tables over was looking at them.

"Well, I'm sorry that you're upset," he said calmly. "But I

don't think I should have to pay full price for a beef dish with no beef."

"Then you should have ordered a vegetarian dish that was on the menu," Keisha said with a tone of disgust.

Her alcohol buzz had worn off. This was all too real and maddening.

The waiter returned. "Sir, as I told you before, your request is the first of its kind. I spoke with the manager. Because it's late and we don't want food to go to waste, he has agreed to re-price the entrée with the tofu substitution to twenty-two dollars."

"That will be fine." Rob nodded.

This is anything but fine.

Since it was past 10:00 p.m. and the restaurant was nearly empty, their dinners were served soon after their orders were placed. They ate most of their meal in silence.

"How's your tofu curry?" Keisha eventually asked. *Not that I care, but maybe some conversation will help the time pass.* "Is it as you wanted it to be?"

"Overall it is, but the shitake mushrooms are too sautéed for my liking. Would you like to try some?" Rob asked. He extended his fork with a piece of tofu on it toward her.

"No, thanks," Keisha said. She looked down at her dish and rolled her eyes. *No need to offer him any of my delicious Peking duck.*

The waiter returned after Keisha and Rob finished their entrées and the dishes had been cleared away. When they declined coffee and dessert, he reached into his back pocket for the check holder.

"Thank you for dining with us this evening." He placed it on the table to the right of Rob and walked away. Rob instantly put his hand on top of the black holder and slid it across the table, parking it dead center in front of Keisha.

"How'd you like to treat me?" he asked in a carefree, friendly manner.

Keisha's jaw dropped. She sat speechless, staring at him with widened eyes. Gradually, she looked down at the check holder. Then back at him. Then back at the check holder. Her brain was having trouble processing Rob's question. Logic and reason weren't kicking in.

After at least half a minute had passed, Keisha heard herself mumble, "Uh-huh, okay, all right."

"Thanks a lot," Rob said. "I'm going to go to the bathroom. I'll be back." He got up and walked across the restaurant to the restroom.

Keisha went through the motions of giving her credit card to the waiter, calculating out the tip, and signing the bill.

Damn! I should have told that cheapskate that I'd split the bill instead of agreeing to pay it all myself. Everything was so muddled. My mind is clearer now.

Well, at least he saved me five dollars. She laughed and shook her head.

When Keisha saw Rob returning to their table, she grabbed her coat and purse and rose from her chair.

"Shall we go?" she asked as she passed him on her way to the front door. He turned and followed.

There was silence between them as they walked down the alleyway to the main street. Where the streets met sat a homeless man on the sidewalk. He had an empty coffee cup next to him.

Rob pulled out his wallet and removed some money. Kneeling down, he placed the cash in the man's cup.

"Thanks," the man said. Keisha watched, dumbfounded. She was surprised that a guy who was so money conscious on a date would freely hand over cash to someone he didn't know in need.

"Sure thing," Rob said. Then he turned to Keisha. "I had a really nice time tonight."

I bet you did. There's nothing like a free dinner.

"I'm glad. And thanks for the drinks," she replied. Her voice was devoid of emotion. "Have a good rest of your night." Keisha turned and began the three-block walk up the street to her parked car.

"Okay, you too. I'll call you," Keisha heard him call out behind her. She kept walking.

The Rest of the Story

The following day, Keisha was working late at the office when she noticed a voice mail on her cell phone from a number she didn't recognize. She pressed "play." It was Rob. He had called to ask her out.

This guy is clueless. There's no way I'm going out with him again.

Keisha had recapped all that had happened on the date with four of her girlfriends. They'd all agreed she'd gotten off easy and there'd be no date number two.

Instead of calling Rob back, Keisha slid her chair over to her keyboard and typed an e-mail. She didn't want it to be harsh, but she didn't want to leave any question in his mind as to where she stood.

Rob,

> *I got your voice mail. I enjoyed the laughs the other night and it was nice to spend time with you. Thanks for the invite to get together again. However, honestly, I just don't think that things would work out with the two of us. Know that I wish you only the best.*
> > *Take care,*
> > *Keisha*

Keisha pressed "send" and went back to doing her work.

An e-mail from Rob awaited Keisha's return from lunch the next day.

Keisha,

> *Thank you for your message. One of the qualities I sensed about you is your graciousness—something I appreciate very much.*
> > *For what it's worth, I don't disagree with you. It is unlikely that things would work out between the two of us. Perhaps a defining difference between us is that—at least for me—I'm not sure that much matters at this point. From a mere statistical standpoint, I recognize that the odds are against us (or anyone that we might meet), and that if—for whatever reason—we were more easily attachable, then we likely would have been committed at this point in time in our lives. So, even before getting to know you in greater depth, I was well aware of*

the obstacles and the difficulties inherent in any further exploration, whatever their origin may have been. That we have gone on one date is not lost on me, however.

I appreciate that your opinion is based on more than probability, and I don't necessarily disagree with you regarding our future prospects based on the plotted projectile of our first post-introduction encounter. Sure, there are things that I wish would have been different. There are things I wish I had done differently. First dates are a funny animal—perhaps dating in general is. I take it with a grain of salt.

And that's one of the reasons why I don't frontload my judgments in the dating realm—particularly as I get older. Sure, most of the time it won't work out, and much of the time, the discovery process is simply confirmation that my initial impression was accurate. But sometimes there is something that I can't see from the outset. If there is something worthwhile, I don't mind the exploration.

In any event, I am not trying to convince you to change your mind—just sharing with you my thought process. Far be it for me to attempt to do so. It's not my style. That said, should you ever want to be in contact, you are welcome. The pleasure was mine.

I wish you the very best, Rob

Keisha leaned back in her chair and chuckled. *He's truly one of a kind!*

She sat up, took her mouse, and filed his e-mail away in her "Dated and Done" folder.

Keisha and Rob never crossed paths again.

Dating Takeaway Tips

WHO PAYS ON A FIRST DATE? THERE'S NO UNIVERSAL ANSWER.

This aspect of first date etiquette has become a gray area in modern dating. Gone are the days when the hard and fast rule was that the man picks up the bill. Some women are comfortable with this change. Others are not.

This confusion is a by-product of today's age of evolving gender roles and technology-based dating. Dating apps have made it easier to set up and go out on first dates, which can get expensive. Men who date regularly and always foot the bill can get priced out of dating. This is especially true in expensive cities. They may even begin to feel resentful for this implicit expectation.

There are women who feel strongly that the man should always pay for the first date, no exceptions. They may be traditionalists or want to find out if their date is chivalrous. Other women take a more business transactional approach and believe that the person who does the asking out should pay. Then there are women who prefer to split the bill, setting an equitable dynamic with their date right out of the gate. Still other women opt to pick up the entire cost of a first date so that it's clear to the man that there are no strings attached, and no real or perceived debt to be paid.

One way to minimize or eliminate the awkwardness of who pays for the first date is to choose an inexpensive outing, such as taking a walk or meeting for coffee. If something needs to be paid for and your date insists on covering it, offer to treat him the next time. (This presumes you want there to be a "next time.") Take turns. Many men appreciate the kindness in being treated, and it signals that you are seeking a partnership of equals.

Here's the bottom line: You need to decide what's right for you. Pay for all of it or split the bill if you want to. Don't make the move for the check if you feel your date should take care of it. And, if by not doing "the reach" you find yourself in a "check standoff," you will have learned something about him. After all, discovery is what a first date is all about.

DON'T OVERDO IT WITH ALCOHOL

Meeting for a drink is one of the most popular things to do on a first date. Unless you've had substance abuse issues in the past, bars can be fun places to hang out. You get to enjoy a cocktail, beer, or a glass of wine, and the alcohol may help rid you of any pesky jitters you're feeling.

The key is not to overdo it. It's best not to get seriously buzzed or drunk. Is this reminding you of all those warnings you heard in high school? You may feel like you're having fun, but you're on a date to meet a new person, and that's not happening if you're not fully present. You won't learn anything meaningful about your date, and he won't get to know the true you.

Instead, you might lose control and act in ways that don't represent who you truly are. You might even put yourself in harm's way. At least Keisha realized that she'd had too much to drink and shouldn't be driving. Pay attention to how much you drink. More isn't better.

"I went on a date recently and the guy took me horseback riding. That was kind of fun, until we ran out of quarters."

— *Susie Loucks*

artist and comedienne

The Day Trip

*I*t was a nondescript afternoon in early November when Jennifer's office phone rang. The caller ID number wasn't familiar to her, but she answered anyway. She recognized Mark's voice immediately. They'd known each other since they were kids but weren't regularly in touch.

"Hi! What a surprise. How are you?" Jennifer asked.

"I wasn't back for Rosh Hashanah," Mark said after they'd exchanged a few pleasantries, "but I'll be in Denver for Thanksgiving. How about we go skiing that Friday? I remember hearing you're a good skier. It'll give us a chance to catch up since we didn't see each other at synagogue."

Jennifer hesitated. "Okay . . . sure, sounds great. There should be a lot of snow by then." She offered to drive since he wouldn't have a car in town.

"That would be cool," Mark replied. "And I'll pack us a lunch." They finalized their plans and hung up.

That was completely unexpected. How'd he get my number? Then it came to her. They'd exchanged business cards a few years back. She'd thrown his away.

While preparing Thanksgiving dinner, Jennifer mentioned her ski plans with Mark to her mother, to which her mother responded, "Jennifer, maybe you should look at Mark in another way?"

Resurrecting the dismissive tone of voice that she'd mostly abandoned to her adolescent years, Jennifer replied, "Oh, Mom, give me a break. It's Mark. We're *just* going skiing."

❧

Jennifer awoke early that Friday morning. The sky was still pitch-black. She didn't bother to shower since she'd be perspiring on the slopes. It could wait until she got home. Besides, it was just Mark. Again, she dismissed her mom's comment about looking at him in a different way.

As she drove to pick up Mark, she thought back to meeting him in Sunday school when they were both eight. She also recalled the fun they had on the yearbook staff years later when they were seniors in high school. They'd always been acquaintances, but for whatever reason, they hadn't become close friends. The idea of dating Mark had never crossed her mind.

College took them to different states, and they fell out of touch. After graduating, Jennifer returned to Denver and Mark moved east to Chicago. But every fall he flew home during the High Holidays to attend religious services with his father. Both his family and Jennifer's still belonged to the same temple where they'd met in third grade. What began as casual hellos between them turned into annual catch-up conversations either before or after Rosh Hashanah services.

Mark had brought the same girlfriend from Chicago with him twice, and each time, Jennifer had her doubts.

"Annie is nice, but I don't see why he's dating her," she'd told her mom. "She doesn't seem right for him." The observation proved prescient.

The next year, the girlfriend wasn't with Mark. Jennifer was rushing to her car after services had finished when she saw him in the hallway. "Where's Annie?" she asked.

"Oh, we broke up," he responded. "Hey, can you hang out and chat a little?"

"No, sorry, but I can't. My best friend is getting married in three hours. I'm the maid of honor. I've got to go." She gave him a quick hug and raced off.

The following Rosh Hashanah, Jennifer arrived at the synagogue figuring that she and Mark would resume their annual conversation. He never showed up. But here they were, two months later, going skiing. Jennifer was intrigued. They'd never spent time alone. When they hung out at all growing up, it had been with mutual friends. What would their day on the slopes be like?

Mark's dad opened the front door and greeted her with a hug. Mark came down the hallway dressed in a retro, cobalt-blue, one-piece ski suit with pops of green and purple trim. Her lime-green jacket and black ski pants seemed understated in comparison to his colorful attire.

Yikes, that's quite an outfit! At least I won't lose him on the ski slopes! She released an almost imperceptible giggle and then quickly resumed her composure.

Mark placed the boot bag and backpack he'd been carrying on the entry hall floor before also giving her a big hug.

"Great to see you," Mark said. He grabbed the unzipped

backpack. "Have a look." Jennifer peered inside to see a package of chips and clear plastic bags filled with vegetables and sandwiches. "I've packed our lunches. I hope you like turkey."

"You're in luck. I do," she said. He'd picked her favorite cold cut.

"We should be back between six and seven," Mark told his father.

Mark's skis and poles were leaning next to the front door. Jennifer took a few steps toward them, with the intention of carrying them to the car. He quickly cut in front of her. "Thanks, but no need to do that. I'll get them."

"All right, if you insist. I'll take your other stuff." Jennifer collected the boot bag and backpack and headed out of the house.

"Have fun, you two," Mark's father called out before closing the front door.

"We will. Bye!" Jennifer responded over her shoulder.

Their conversation was nonstop during the nearly one-and-a-half-hour drive up 1-70W to Keystone Ski Resort. Mark was at the tail end of his story about his breakup with Annie when they pulled into the resort's parking lot. As soon as Jennifer turned off the engine, Mark got out of her red Subaru and started removing the skis from the ski rack. A wave of cold air greeted Jennifer as she stepped onto the thin layer of ice that blanketed the pavement. Her nose instantly began to drip. She scoured her jacket and pant pockets for a tissue.

"Hey, I got it," Mark said. He promptly placed the skis down, took a step toward her, and wiped her nose with his leather ski glove.

"Thanks," Jennifer said tentatively.

That was kind of sweet. But what's he doing? Why is he wiping my nose? I'm not a child.

Jennifer watched, dumbfounded, as Mark walked over to the snow embankment next to the car and rubbed the soiled glove along its wet surface. He turned back toward her, smiling.

The site of Mark's joyful, magnetic smile eased Jennifer out of her confused daze. *Come to think of it, he's always had the reputation for being a considerate guy.*

"Tell you what, I'll get the skis. How about you take the poles?" Mark asked, seemingly oblivious to Jennifer's bewilderment. Without waiting for her to reply, he started across the snow-rimmed parking lot.

"Ah, okay, sure," Jennifer stuttered. She locked the car, picked up both sets of poles, and hurried to catch up with him.

No guy had ever carried her skis for her, not even an ex-boyfriend. Mark, however, had packed her a lunch, wiped her nose, and was now carrying her skis.

What in the world's going on? Is this just him being thoughtful, or does he want to be more than friends?

They each paid for their lift ticket and got in line to take the gondola up Dercum Mountain. The queue moved quickly. When it came time for them to board the six-seater gondola, Jennifer stepped in, placed the four poles against the cabin's side wall, and sat on the bench facing up the mountain. She'd learned years earlier that she was likely to get altitude sickness if she didn't sit looking up at the mountain as the gondola ascended. She didn't want to get nauseated and disrupt their day trip. Mark sat down on the village-facing bench, took off his ski gloves, and placed them in his lap.

As the gondola began to climb, Jennifer was transfixed by the winter wonderland around them. A series of storms had swept through the Rockies during the previous two weeks, and snow still blanketed most of the tree branches and rooftops that lined Keystone Village.

"It's such a gorgeous view," Mark said after a minute of silence had passed.

"I agree. There is so much snow. It's *so* pretty!" Jennifer replied as she gazed through the window to her right.

"No, I wasn't talking about *that* view," Mark said.

His words awoke Jennifer from her tranquil state, and she turned her head toward Mark abruptly. The ear-to-ear smile emblazoned on his face was impossible to miss. She just stared at him. Were it not for her polarized goggles, he'd have surely noticed her raised eyebrows and widened eyes. Jennifer gradually felt a wave of warmth pass over her cheeks. The surprise-induced tightness in her jaw relaxed, and a full-blown smile emerged.

"Thanks, Mark," she heard herself say. Jennifer looked back out the window, hoping that he hadn't seen her blushing.

What just happened? Could my mom have been onto something? Jennifer tried to picture herself on Mark's arm instead of Annie. *I'm not sure. Maybe?*

"Where should we start off skiing?" she asked, as though nothing out of the ordinary had just happened.

Her question sparked a conversation that veered from their favorite ski slopes at the resort, to tales about the last time each of them had skied at Keystone, to how they each learned to ski as kids. They continued chatting as they disembarked the gondola, snapped on their skis, and whisked down the hillside to the lift below.

Jennifer and Mark spent the day traversing the ski runs. From time to time, they'd stop to talk on the slopes as they made their descent. During one break, they chitchatted for such a long time that Jennifer got antsy.

"C'mon, let's ski, and we'll talk on the way!" she declared and took off down the mountain. Mark had to catch up to complete his sentence. Their banter continued as they skied side by side.

Jennifer and Mark waited for the lunch crowd to return to the slopes before taking a break. Once inside the lodge, Mark pulled out the lunches that he'd been carrying in his backpack.

He does have beautiful hazel eyes, she thought as she munched on her sandwich. He hardly broke eye contact once. It made her feel as if he was truly interested in whatever she said. And the warmth in his gaze made him seem so caring and honest. They ate their meals quickly, so as not to miss out on much ski time.

Jennifer glanced over at Mark as they were putting their helmets back on. She liked how the hints of blond lightened his brown hair, and the way it fell over his forehead.

He actually looks a little like Daniel Radcliffe.

Back on the slopes that afternoon, Jennifer and Mark stopped to admire the magnificent view of the peaks. Rays of sunlight piercing through the cloudy sky lit many of the snow-covered summits that dotted the horizon. Jennifer turned away from the stunning panorama to say something to Mark when he unexpectedly leaned over and kissed her tenderly. Instead of closing her eyes, Jennifer widened them, surprised by the bold move. They stood silently, smiling at each other for a few moments and relishing a first kiss that had unexpectedly been more than twenty-five years in the making.

She hadn't seen it coming, but it was feeling better than okay.

I'll journal about it later and think it through then. For now, I'm living in the moment!

Jennifer caught Mark by surprise when she suddenly pushed off on her poles and took off down the run. Again, she called back jovially, "C'mon, let's ski, and we'll talk on the way!"

They flirted on and off that afternoon, holding hands on the chairlift and stealing kisses occasionally.

"Why didn't we ever date in high school?" Mark asked on one of their chairlift rides.

"It was probably because we were off doing our own things," she said. "And please don't be offended, but I never looked at you that way."

"No offense taken."

They continued to ski until Jennifer noticed that it was close to four o'clock. The lifts would stop running soon.

"I love après-ski," she told him. "Let's get some nachos and beers so we can hang out before we get on the road."

"Après-ski? It hasn't really been my thing," said Mark. "But with you, why not?"

After an hour or so of drinks and snacks in the lodge, they packed up the car and left. Jennifer drove them back to Denver. Mark suggested dinner and she agreed. Over sushi, he asked if she wanted to go see a movie. They chose *Silver Linings Play-*

book. Seated in the dark theater, they held hands throughout the entire film.

Could this movie be more perfect? Jennifer wondered. *This may be the best first date I've ever been on.*

Afterward, she drove Mark back to his dad's house. They sat parked in the driveway for a long time, making out like high schoolers. It remained pretty innocent, especially considering they weren't teenagers any longer.

"I'm flying back to Chicago on Monday," Mark said before getting out of the car. "But I'll be returning over Christmas to go up to my family's place in the mountains, near Edwards. You should come and ski with us."

Jennifer didn't hesitate—she'd had so much fun with him on their unexpected first date. "I'd love to!"

After Jennifer got home, she pulled out her journal and wrote about her day with Mark.

He's such a sweet man. Caring, sensitive, and thoughtful. The bummer is, he doesn't live here. Small glitch. But if we're meant to be together, it will work out.

The Rest of the Story

Jennifer went up to the mountains for a week of skiing and snowshoeing with Mark and his family after Christmas. They spent New Year's Eve together and started the next year off with the "Do you want to have children?" conversation. Both answered "yes."

Their relationship moved along quickly. After Mark returned to Chicago, they e-mailed or talked every day, and they managed to see each other at least every two weeks. That May, Mark's job was relocated to Washington, DC. He asked Jennifer to move there with him. She agreed on the condition that they were engaged. In September, Mark proposed atop a mountain in Vail. Their engagement happened ten months after their first date. Jennifer moved in with Mark soon after, and they were married the following spring.

Today, Mark and Jennifer live in Denver with their two sons. Whenever there's enough snow in the Rockies on the Friday after Thanksgiving, they relive their first date. They ski during the day, go out for a sushi dinner afterward, and finish their evening on the couch at home watching *Silver Linings Playbook*. But what was originally a twosome date has become a foursome outing, with their sons joining them on their anniversary celebration.

Dating Takeaway Tips

DON'T RULE OUT DATING SOMEONE FROM YOUR PAST.

It's natural to have formed opinions about people you met years earlier. We all do it. And although it may not be fair, when we think about people from our school years, we often automatically affix the same label to them that we assigned them decades earlier—they're a geek; they're a stoner. Are you the same person you were in high school? Unless you're *still* in high school, the answer is undoubtedly "no." None of us are.

There's often an inner comfort that comes from spending

time with people we knew earlier in our lives, unless those years were traumatic ones. If you re-meet someone you knew years earlier and sense an attraction to them, or if they want to get to know you anew, be open to it. Temporarily put those judgments from years ago aside and find out if they've evolved into someone who could be a romantic match for you, or a companion whose company you'd enjoy.

LET HIM BE A GENTLEMAN.

You can see the signs of a man's interest in you and his potential to be a thoughtful, kind partner by observing what he does to try to make you happy. Mark made Jennifer lunch, insisted on carrying her skis to the resort, and even wiped her nose! Jennifer's responses to these attempts to please her were perfect, especially considering she's an independent woman who wasn't used to men doing things for her. Even though she was surprised, Jennifer didn't tell Mark, "That's okay, I'll take care of it," when he picked up her skis. Instead, she graciously received his attention, kindness, and help.

Good men need to know that they can enhance your life in some way. If they get the message that you won't allow them to, they will leave. You should know that the opposite is also true: men who would rather *receive* than give are looking for women who want to do everything for themselves. If you're a thoughtful, self-sufficient woman who's a ninja at getting things done, you're likely to attract men who don't want to do things for you. By receiving graciously, you're more likely to attract the good men you want to meet.

"There is no happiness like that of being loved by your fellow creatures, and feeling that your presence is an addition to their comfort."

— *Charlotte Brontë*

author and poet

The Winer

P atricia's iPhone rang as she stepped onto the commuter bus that she rode each night from downtown to her suburban stop. She claimed an empty seat and glanced down at her phone. Philip, her blind date that night, was calling. Patricia tapped "decline," whisking the call to voice mail.

People who talked on their cell phones while on the bus annoyed her. She refused to join their ranks. Patricia texted him instead.

"I'm on the bus and can't talk right now. I will call you as soon as I get to my stop. 15 to 20 minutes, tops."

Her phone rang less than a minute later. It was Philip again. Patricia sent his call to voice mail for a second time. She wondered if his calling an hour before they were to meet meant that the date was off. There was a long to-do list to keep her busy at home if his plans had changed.

"I'll call you when I'm off the bus. I look forward to seeing you soon!" her second text read.

Patricia put in her earbuds to hear his voice mail. "Hi, Patricia, Philip here. The phone rang once, but then it went to voice mail. I don't know what happened. Call me when you get this." She didn't.

Instead, she dialed him back as she disembarked from the bus. He answered after one ring.

"Hi, Philip," she said. "This is Patricia. I got your voice mail. Are we still on for tonight?"

When they'd spoken on the phone the week prior, he'd put it to her to come up with a place for them to meet for a drink. "Do you like wine?" she'd asked. A former-wine-salesperson-turned-corporate accountant, she still stayed current on the local wine scene.

"Of course I do," he had said. A self-proclaimed oenophile, she was pleased that they had wine in common. Patricia suggested Les Amis Café. The owners had been her customers years earlier. Their bartenders understood wines, and the café usually stocked high-quality varietals at reasonable prices. Philip assured her he'd been there before, and they agreed to meet at the downstairs bar.

"Yes, we're on for tonight," Philip said, after she asked him if they were still meeting that evening.

"Great!" She picked up the pace, her blue kitten heels hitting the pavement a little faster. She needed to get home and change out of her work clothes before driving to the café. "I don't think Karen showed you a photo of me. When you get to the café, look for a blond, blue-eyed woman with hair a few inches below her shoulders. I'll be wearing a navy-blue blouse and a scarf." A few pleasantries were exchanged, and the call ended.

Patricia and Karen became friends soon after Patricia's marriage ended. The two divorcées, both in their forties, went for power walks in the hills around their homes before work at least once a week. An early riser, Patricia always made it back home in time to see her sons off to school.

While on a Monday morning walk a few weeks earlier, Karen started talking about the guy she'd gone out with that Saturday night.

"Philip is handsome and smart. The guy has a PsyD in psychology, after all. He's successful, too, or at least he comes across that way. He talked a lot about his therapy practice and how busy he is with patients. I asked a lot of questions. Maybe too many, because when we were saying goodbye, he didn't say anything about getting together again."

They reached a plateau on the trail. Karen stopped. She turned to face Patricia, the sun rising over the horizon behind her.

"Guys who want to see a woman again always say something at the end of the date, or at least hint that they're interested." Karen paused to take in the beauty of the sunrise before her. "At first I was bummed, but I was thinking about it last night, and I have a feeling that you and Philip might hit it off. How about I set you up with him?"

"Really? What makes you think that we could be a match?" Patricia asked.

"Well, it's more of a gut thing—women's intuition," Karen said. "You have a lot in common. You're both smart, care about living healthy, and are good at what you do. That doesn't guarantee that he's the man for you, but these things do count for a lot. And I think the two of you together would make a very good-looking couple!"

After a little more prodding by Karen, Patricia agreed to the introduction. It had been two months since her last date. The profiles of the guys that eHarmony had been e-mailing her lately were not the least bit intriguing.

Why not meet Philip? I trust Karen's intuition.

Karen took on her role of matchmaker with zeal. On the way down the hill, she texted Philip. He texted her back that night, agreeing to the date and asking for Patricia's number. The next evening, Philip and Patricia spoke, and he asked her out.

Patricia walked into Les Amis and looked around. No men were seated alone. She spotted an empty table directly in front of the main door. Patricia placed her clutch on the cherrywood table-top, hung her wool jacket on the nearby coat rack, and sat down. She adjusted her Pucci scarf to lie flat over her shoulders. He'd have to walk past her table to get to the bar, so it would be hard for them to miss one another when Philip came in. Her watch read 6:55 p.m. Patricia liked to arrive a few minutes early.

The waitress brought her water and a drink menu. Patricia held off ordering a glass of wine. Philip would be arriving shortly, after all. But when 7:05 p.m. turned into 7:15 p.m. and he still hadn't shown up, she got concerned.

"Hi. Where are you?" Patricia asked as soon as Philip answered his cell phone. "Are you still coming? I'm downstairs at the bar at Les Amis."

"Oh, I'm downstairs at the bar at the Hanley Hotel," he responded.

"You are? What are you doing there? We said Les Amis."

"Yeah, maybe. I thought we said the Hanley. I could swear that's what we said," Philip responded. "But since you're at Les Amis, I won't ask you to come here. I should be there in fifteen minutes."

Patricia placed the phone on the table and gradually sat back into the wooden chair. Replaying in her mind all her back and forth with Philip, she couldn't remember the Hanley Hotel ever being mentioned as a possible meeting spot.

We all forget things. He's probably had a rough day at work.

Patricia ordered a glass of nebbiolo to help pass the time. She'd just taken her third sip when a tall, coatless man in his midforties walked in. His sheer white linen shirt accentuated his tanned complexion and thinly veiled his toned abs and sculpted arms. Patricia wasn't used to seeing people sporting such bronzed skin in November.

She rose as the handsome, well-groomed man approached. "You must be Patricia," he said.

"Yes, I am," she replied, shaking his hand. Patricia picked up a whiff of aftershave. Not the strong scented type that her ex-boyfriend wore. Whatever Philip's was had a subtler sandalwood aroma. She put him at six feet to her five-foot-eight height.

"I'm thankful the planning stuff is behind us," Philip said. He pulled out the chair to her right and sat down.

"Me too," she said as she sat. "After the extra driving you did, you're probably thirsty. How about we get you a glass of wine?"

"That's the best idea I've heard all day." He swung his head toward the mostly empty tables behind them. Spotting a wait-ress across the room, he waved his hand in the air to get her attention. "Hey, we'd like some service over here," Philip called out.

The waitress walked over. "Hi, what can I get you?"

"I know we have a wine menu sitting right there, but how about you make a recommendation? I can tell you know a lot about wines," he said. "I like my wine sweet. What do you think I should drink?"

"Well, two wines come to mind," she said. "One is a fruit-forward zinfandel, and the other is a dessert wine."

"Since it's not dessert time yet, I'll have the zin."

"Terrific. I'll be back with your wine soon." The waitress left the menu where it lay on the table and headed over to the bar. Philip turned to face Patricia. "So, tell me about you. Have you been married? Do you have kids?"

"Yes, I've been married. And now I have a 'was-band,' Sam," she replied.

Philip slammed his left hand on the table and let out a chuckle. "A was-band? I love it!"

"Thanks, I came up with the term. My ex doesn't mind it. Sam and I have been divorced for just over five years, but it's im-portant to both of us to keep a good relationship because of our sons." Patricia was momentarily distracted by Philip's uniformly rich hazel eyes.

This guy has gorgeous eyes. Maybe too perfect. I wonder if the color is natural, or if he has lenses in? She took a sip of wine.

"Anthony is in high school, and Timothy is in middle school. With all the challenges that go on in those years of a boy's life, the last thing they need are parents who bicker."

Taking another sip of her wine, Patricia observed that Philip's shirtsleeves clung tightly to his accentuated biceps. *Clearly this guy spends a lot of time in the gym. If he gets any more muscular, that fabric is going to tear.*

Patricia placed her glass back on the table. "Sam lives across the street from us in his mother's house, so the boys see their dad a lot. He's already been remarried and divorced. That took all of two years. How about you? Have any ex-wives? Kids?"

"I have something in common with Sam," Philip said. "I'm also two women's was-band. My second marriage lasted around two years. I met Avery, my first, a few years after finishing grad school. She was originally from Texas too. Got my undergrad degree at the University of Texas. Moved here from San Antonio to get my PsyD in clinical psychology. I stayed, and now I've got my own practice. Maybe Karen told you?"

"She didn't tell me too much," Patricia said. "I think she wanted us to learn about each other on our own."

"Yeah, probably. I wish I had learned a lot more about my two exes before I married them. The first turned out to be a real pain, always telling me what to do. Like I don't have a brain of my own?" Philip glanced over at the bar. "She wasn't like that at first. That marriage lasted for six long years. I thank the high heavens that I only had to pay her alimony for that amount of time. She's out of my life now. What a relief! No kids with her. Then there was number two, Sandra. No kids with her either."

Two divorces and lots of resentment; I'd like to hear how his former wives describe him.

The waitress arrived and removed a glass from the full tray

she was skillfully balancing. "Here's your wine," she said, carefully depositing it before him.

She ambled off toward a table nearby where a group of women in their twenties had just been seated. Philip took a sip. "Blech!" he said loudly. He put the glass down and abruptly called out to the waitress, "Come here, you!"

Patricia's genial gaze at Philip transformed into a glare. The intensity of her stare increased the longer she looked at him. It was only when her eyes started to tear up that she realized she needed to blink.

How dare this numbskull treat the waitress so rudely!

The women at the neighboring table halted their conversations and looked over at Philip. Patricia read expressions of disbelief and disgust on their faces. The waitress didn't waver. She continued to serve the women their wine glasses like nothing out of the ordinary had happened. "I'll be right there," she casually replied to his summons.

Philip began berating her as soon as she walked over. "I told you I wanted a sweet wine. This is not a sweet wine." Patricia looked downward to avoid eye contact with the waitress.

"Okay, if this wine is not to your liking, how about trying a dessert wine?" the waitress replied, maintaining her friendly tone of voice. "We have a French Banyuls or a Sauterne that you might like."

"I want to try them both," he responded.

"No problem." She picked up the rejected glass of wine and departed for the bar.

"Okay, where was I?" Philip asked, his voice reverting to its previous friendly tone. "Ah yes, back to Sandra. You sort of look alike—the blond hair and blue eyes. But her hair was longer. It went down below her shoulders. I liked it when she wore it up. It was sexy."

"Good to know," Patricia said, hoping that he'd pick up on her sarcasm. "How could you be so rude to a waitress? That wasn't called for."

"I was the one who was wrong? Me?" Philip asked indignantly. "Hey, it was wrong of *her* to bring me wine that didn't taste the way I explicitly told her I wanted it to. She's the expert. She gave the recommendation. I just want what I want."

The waitress soon returned to the table and set two glasses, with tasting-size pours, down in front of Philip.

"This is the Banyuls and this is the Sauterne for you to try," she said, pointing first to the glass on the right and then to the one on the left. "I'll be back after you've had a chance to sample them."

As the waitress turned, Philip extended his left arm, blocking her from moving forward. "Don't go anywhere yet," he said as he picked up the first glass with his right hand. The waitress stopped and looked at him incredulously.

"This one is to my satisfaction," Philip said, pointing to the Sauterne. He lowered his left arm.

"So, I can go now?" the waitress asked brusquely.

Her congenial demeanor had wilted away. He nodded and she left.

Patricia's stare returned. She was speechless. Philip, oblivious to her reaction, was busy checking something on his phone.

This guy is awful. I should get up and walk out right now. But I do like the food here. Why should I be the one to leave?

Patricia was distracted from her thoughts upon hearing her name called out from across the room. She looked over at the staircase to see Robert, the co-owner of the café, walking down from the restaurant on the second floor. She smiled and waved him over. Noticing that Patricia had stood up, Philip put his phone down and stood as well.

"It's great to see you, Patricia. It's been too long," Robert said. They hugged. Her anger was extinguished by the delight of seeing her old acquaintance.

"Yes, it has been. I miss our regular wine talks. You were a tough negotiator, but one of my favorite clients," she said.

She didn't want to introduce him to Philip, but it would have been incredibly awkward if she didn't, given that the guy was standing right there.

"Robert, I'd like you to meet Philip Miller," Patricia said, maintaining her smile as best she could.

"That's *Doctor* Philip Miller," he said as they shook hands. Patricia winced.

"I see," Robert said warily. "What kind of doctor are you?"

"I'm a clinical psychologist. My private practice treats kids and adults with mental health issues, abnormal behavior, and psychiatric problems."

His pompous tone grated on her, and she couldn't hold back from unleashing a bit of sarcasm.

"You must know a lot about those topics," Patricia said. "For you to have earned your doctorate, I mean. And to have your own practice and all."

Philip crossed his arms, puffing up even more.

"Actually, I do," he said. "It wasn't easy. First, I had to get my undergrad degree and then my master's and doctorate. I did an internship, spent two years in a clinical training program, and then had to pass both the Professional Practice in Psychology exam and the state's exam."

"That must have been a lot of hard work," Robert said. He glanced at Patricia, his eyes widening. Patricia was eager to respond with a wink but didn't. Philip hadn't picked up on her sarcasm, but he might notice *that* not-so-subtle exchange.

"It was." Philip began rocking back and forth on his heels. "But it's all been worth it, helping my patients and all. My mom is a psychiatrist. While not quite the same thing, she's been my professional inspiration."

"It's always nice to meet a doctor," Robert said cordially. Turning to Patricia, he lightly placed his hand on her left shoulder. "Again, it's great to see you, Patricia. You two enjoy your evening. I've got to get back to work."

Patricia and Philip sat back down. Philip took another sip of wine. Sitting silently, Patricia's attention turned to the remix of Ray Charles's "Hit the Road Jack" that was playing overhead. It was music to her ears.

"I need to go to the ladies' room." She stood up and reached for her purse, placing it under her arm. Then she turned to Philip, who remained seated. "Since I haven't had dinner and it's getting later, when I return, I'm going to order some food at the bar. Please don't feel that you're committed to having anything more than a drink with me."

"Okay, but wait a second. I haven't even seen all of you yet," Philip said. "Step back and turn around so I can see you." He made a circular motion with his index finger.

"Absolutely not! I'm not going to do that," Patricia responded, glaring at him. *What a jerk!*

She turned on her heel and walked briskly to the restroom. There she lingered, powdering her nose, applying fresh lipstick, checking e-mail, and scanning posts on Facebook. The longer she took, the more likely it was that Philip would be done with his wine when she returned.

Her calculation was spot-on. Philip's credit card had already been run when Patricia rejoined him. He signed the bill and stood up. "I get the impression that you're not going to want to get together again. But if you do, here's my card." He handed it to her. She took it and slid it into her purse's side pocket.

"Thanks for the drink. And don't get a chill out there," Patricia said with an almost imperceptible smirk.

"I'll be fine," he said. She watched as Philip walked out the door with only his thin linen shirt and jeans to protect him from the cold winter night.

The waitress who had served them was wiping down the countertop at the end of the bar. Patricia walked over and sat on a stool in front of her.

"I'm so sorry and embarrassed that my date treated you rudely. I feel awful about it. It was a blind date."

"Don't you worry," the waitress said. She stopped cleaning, the damp cloth lingering in her right hand. "It wasn't your fault. You only just met him. How people treat servers is a great indicator of what kind of people they are. And based on the way he spoke to me, the guy's a jerk."

"How right you are," Patricia said. "The man is a nightmare! No wonder he's had two failed marriages."

"Why am I not surprised? Good thing you quickly realized what it took those other two women longer to figure out," the waitress said. "Tell you what. After surviving a date with *that* guy, I think you've earned another drink. This one's on the house."

"That is so nice of you!" Patricia said. "For some reason, spending time with him has made me hungry." The waitress picked up one of the dinner menus from behind the bar and laid it down before Patricia.

After placing her order, Patricia tasted the glass of pinot noir from Anderson Valley that the waitress had just poured.

"Outstanding choice," she told the waitress. "Forget what that guy said. You do know your wines. Thanks again."

Robert approached. "Did everything go okay there?" he asked. "That guy correcting you because you didn't mention that he was a doctor was completely out of line. He wasn't even a medical doctor, was he?"

"Ah, no, he was not," Patricia said. "I have a friend to thank for that introduction. Or maybe she isn't as good a friend as I had thought she was." Patricia and Robert laughed.

Their laughter trailed off, and she took another sip.

"You and I should have gone out. We would have had a much better time," a deep voice behind her said.

Patricia swiveled her stool around to see a gray-haired man in his late fifties seated at a table a few feet away. He was wearing a half-zip Polo sweater, and the sweater's chambray color made his blue eyes stand out. He was flanked by two well-dressed, college-aged women.

"Really?" Patricia asked the man playfully. "You know how to show a woman a good time?" All five of them laughed.

"I certainly do. I'm an old-school gentleman. My daughters will back me up on this."

"Believe it or not, he is," the older of the two brunette women said. "If being an old-school gentleman means opening doors for women, pulling out our chairs, and having us leave the elevator before he does, that is."

"Sounds about right to me." Patricia got off her stool and walked over. "I'm Patricia."

"I'm Milt," he said, standing up to shake her hand. They exchanged cards.

"Give me a call sometime, if you'd like," Patricia said.

"That I'll do," he responded.

Patricia smiled. "I'll look forward to it."

Milt took his seat and Patricia returned to her barstool, where she enjoyed the rest of her glass of wine and the entrée that had just been served.

The Rest of the Story

Milt called Patricia a few days later and asked her out. Their date was to a public concert in a local park. They had a pleasant time but agreed that their fifteen-year age difference was too wide a gap for a romantic relationship to flourish.

Patricia was disappointed in Karen's judgment. It became clear to her that the qualities and values that they were looking for in men were vastly different. However, Patricia decided not to make a big deal about the failed date with Karen. She didn't return the favor by setting her friend up with Milt, nor did she ever see Philip again.

Dating Takeaway Tips

MAKE SURE YOU'RE RESPECTED.

If you're out with a man and he starts speaking badly about other women he's dated or been married to, beware! This could be a warning sign that he isn't respectful of others, especially women. Don't go down a slippery slope with someone like this. If you're in a long-term relationship with a person who treats you like less than his equal, in time your self-esteem will decrease from the bruising it's withstood. You will have compromised the most important relationship in your life—the one you have with yourself!

YOU DON'T HAVE TO LEAVE. HE CAN.

You can recover from a bad date that very afternoon or evening. If you're enjoying your surroundings but not the company, you don't have to be the one to leave—your date can. Patricia wanted to have dinner at Les Amis Café, but not with Philip. She politely laid out her plans to him. She would be staying for dinner, and he was not invited to join her. She was cordial, courteous, and to the point. After he left, her evening took a positive turn that she never could have anticipated. If you find yourself in similar circumstances, hold your ground, and do what Patricia did.

"How you feel about yourself is how you live."

— *Anonymous*

The Dame in Shining Armor

*N*o one was waiting for her at the hostess desk when Julie arrived at the restaurant. She quickly scanned the main dining room at P.F. Chang's to see if Steve had already been seated. He wasn't there.

"Table for two, please. We don't have a reservation," Julie said. She felt her heart racing. The hostess smiled at Julie and checked an iPad to review the restaurant's seating layout.

"Not a problem. Right this way." She picked up two menus and headed toward the dining room. Julie followed her across the room and through the double doors that led outside. The hostess stopped in the middle of the back patio.

"How's this table?" she asked. It was a warm October evening, and it was quieter outside than in the main dining room.

"It will be fine. Thanks," she replied.

Julie hung her jacket on the chair, placed her purse on the ground and phone on the table, and sat down.

It was her first time dining at P.F. Chang's. When Steve called and asked her out on a dinner date, he'd insisted that *she* pick the restaurant.

"Anywhere you want," he'd said. Julie had been eager to try P.F. Chang's. Tonight was the night.

It was a safe choice. She knew that Steve liked Asian food. He'd ordered it for a lunchtime baby shower he'd hosted for a colleague on his finance team. Even though Julie hadn't worked in his department, the mother-to-be was her friend and had invited her. She'd also been Steve's human resource counterpart on a few cross-functional projects. They'd become friendly, the kind of coworkers who exchanged more than pleasantries but not so close that they made plans outside of work.

There'd been that one evening when they were both working late. Steve had walked into Julie's office and suggested they grab dinner. She'd declined since she'd brought her meal and had already eaten it.

Steve's proposition got Julie thinking about whether he was someone she'd want to date. They were both single and in their late thirties. Steve was friendly and easy to talk to, with a wry sense of humor. He had a strong pedigree, the son of a well-respected doctor. Having been raised in a Catholic family, Steve had gone to a Jesuit university for both his undergraduate and graduate degrees.

He wasn't handsome in the conventional *GQ* magazine sense. A stocky man, Steve would be completely bald were it not for the hair donut that wrapped around his head from ear to ear. Yet Julie was attracted to the way he carried himself and the confidence he exuded. Plus, she was partial to men with blue eyes.

But since there'd been no invitation to dinner, or any other activity, in the following months, Julie had dismissed the prospect. She'd placed him firmly in the "work friend" category.

That designation didn't change after Steve left the company six months ago for a controller job elsewhere. He'd stayed in touch, occasionally sending her lighthearted e-mails and texts. There was no hint in any of their interactions that he was interested in her romantically. Then, out of the blue, he called her on Monday and asked her out.

Julie had just begun reading through the menu when the waitress approached, welcomed her, and asked whether she'd like something to drink. Julie decided to stick with dating etiquette and wait for Steve to arrive before ordering.

"I'm meeting a friend. Water will be fine for now."

She resumed studying the extensive dinner menu. The restaurant served two of her favorite Chinese dishes, chicken lettuce wraps and beef with broccoli. There were plenty of other items that whet her appetite too. She read each description. After perusing the entire menu, Julie looked at her watch. Steve was fifteen minutes late. She got out of her chair, walked to the dining room doorway, and peered inside. Julie didn't see him seated anywhere and returned to her table. The waitress came by as Julie pulled her chair in.

"Would you like a drink other than water? How about we get some starters going?" Fearing that yawns could soon set in, Julie ordered a Coke.

She read through the menu a second time and then a third. Julie picked up her phone and checked Instagram. She scanned her favorite news sites, regularly glancing over at the double doors. She tapped her foot, unable to concentrate on the articles she was reading. *Has something happened to Steve?*

As the people seated at the surrounding tables were being

served their meals, Julie kept her eyes focused downward on her phone. She hoped that the other diners wouldn't notice her sitting across from an empty place setting. Julie slowly sipped her Coke. Another fifteen minutes went by. Her phone hadn't rung, and there was no text from Steve.

Could he have forgotten about our plans?

The waitress reappeared with a pitcher in hand.

"Your Coke could do for a refill," she said. Julie nodded. The waitress poured more soda into Julie's glass. "Do you want to order some food?"

Julie glanced at her phone sitting idly by. Then she picked up the menu and started casually flipping through it. "My friend will probably be arriving soon. So yes, I'm going to go ahead and order. We'll take the chicken lettuce wraps, beef with broccoli, and the surf and turf."

"Very good." The waitress finished writing up the order, closed her notepad, and left.

Julie picked up her phone. She read more news stories and bounced between apps that she rarely opened. Every few minutes she looked back at the double doors. Her stomach rumbled. She tried to ignore it. Another fifteen minutes passed.

Where is he? I've waited long enough! Julie scrolled through her contacts and tapped on Steve's phone number. He picked up after the second ring.

"Hey, I'm here at P.F. Chang's and you're not. Did you forget that we are getting together tonight?"

"No, I didn't forget. I'm tied up at work," Steve replied in the same nonchalant tone she'd heard him use when he'd ask, "How's it going?" as they passed by one another at work.

"Really?" Julie asked. "You're tied up at work? You could have called me. I've been waiting here for forty-five minutes!"

"Uh . . . I'm sorry about that. Work was awful today. I've got lots to do. I don't think I can make it. I'll call you later." There was silence on the line. Steve had hung up.

Julie was motionless, frozen in place. Her thoughts and senses went numb as the scene before her turned blurry. The conversations that surrounded her, and the music piped in overhead, were muffled. Time stood still.

She was awoken from her daze by the pungent scent of hoisin sauce. Julie looked down slowly. The plate of chicken lettuce wraps had been served. Gradually, she lowered the phone from where it rested against her right ear, placed it on the table, and stared at the food.

I hate this familiar feeling. Is there something wrong with me? Why would Steve do this to me?

The scene around her gradually came back into view: the two women across from her were laughing as they ate their desserts, the mother of a family of four was scooping rice onto the plates of her preteen kids, a couple to Julie's right were holding hands across the table as they awaited their meal.

Julie looked at the vacant chair across from her. The servers would be back soon with the other two dishes she'd ordered. Her head drooped.

After a few minutes, she picked up her phone, tapped on her list of recent calls, and selected Samantha's number. The two had talked during the entirety of Julie's drive from her office to the restaurant. Julie didn't bother to say hello.

"Steve's not here. He's not coming," she said, fighting back tears. "I'm very embarrassed and ashamed. And I've already ordered food. I don't know what to do."

"Stay right where you are," Samantha said. "I'm coming!"

Julie put the phone back on the table and placed her elbow down next to it. With her hand partially shielding her face, Julie attempted to hide in plain sight. She closed her eyes and replayed the conversation with Steve. She was struck by the cavalier way he had spoken to her.

How could he humiliate me like this? Why did he ask me out in the first place?

Julie felt her belly rumble again. She opened her eyes, took her fork, and began picking at the pile of lettuce and mound of chicken. All the while, her hand was shielding her eyes from the people surrounding her.

"Julie, there you are! I'm so sorry that I'm incredibly late!" a loud, familiar voice called out.

She jolted upright. Samantha was heading across the patio toward her.

"I can't believe I made you wait *so* long!" Samantha declared at a volume more appropriate for a loud sports stadium than a restaurant. "You're such a good friend to be so patient. Again, I'm very sorry!"

Julie stood up and gave her friend a hug. She noticed that the couple was watching them. "How's that for an entrance?" Samantha whispered in Julie's ear as they embraced.

"Thank you. You're the best," Julie replied softly with a half-hearted smile.

Samantha had just sat down when the waitress appeared holding the two other dishes Julie had ordered.

"*You're* the one she's been waiting for?" the waitress asked Samantha. Julie heard surprise and skepticism in the server's voice.

"Why, yes, I am. I got tied up at work. Things were crazy today!"

The waitress hesitated a moment. "Okay, then." She nodded slightly before returning to her station.

Samantha served food onto both of their plates. "You need to eat this before it gets cold," she said. "Now, tell me everything that happened."

Julie started eating in earnest as she ran through the recap. She recounted her brief conversation with Steve word for word.

"I want to call him again," Julie said after finishing her story.

Samantha stopped eating and abruptly put her fork down.

"No, you don't. Don't call him. That's an *awful* idea. He's a horrible person for doing this to you. You can't call him."

"You're probably right," Julie replied with a sigh.

They talked for a while about how hurt and depressed Steve's treatment of Julie made her feel. "Enough of this for now," Julie said. She placed her napkin on the table. "I need to use the restroom. I'll be back."

She stood up, grabbed her purse, and headed toward the main dining room. While continuing to eat, Samantha noticed that Julie had left her phone behind. She picked it up, went to the recent call list, and tapped on the phone number below hers.

"Hello," a man's voice said.

"I'm Samantha, Julie's friend. I'm calling to tell you that you're an asshole. You didn't show up, and you left her sitting alone at the restaurant!"

Steve cleared his throat. "Yes, I guess I am. But I did stop by. I walked into the restaurant and looked for Julie. When I didn't see her, I took off."

"Did you check the patio?"

"Uh, no, I didn't."

"Did you even call?"

"No."

"You're such a dick. Don't ever call Julie again."

Steve paused. "Okay, I won't."

Samantha hung up the phone and placed it back where Julie had left it. She resumed eating her meal.

After Julie returned from the restroom, Samantha remarked nonchalantly, "I called Steve and told him he was an asshole."

"What? You did what?" Julie let out a few laughs. As they trailed off, she reverted to a more solemn state. "What did he say?"

"He said that he came by the restaurant, looked in, didn't see you, and left."

Julie shook her head. "You've got to be kidding! Where did he look? Why didn't he see me?"

"I have no idea, and I'm not sure I believe him," Samantha said. "But at this point, does it really matter?"

"No, it doesn't," Julie said. Her head drooped again. "It's just that I always took Steve to be a good Catholic man."

"I know. And there are 'good Catholic men' out there. He's just not one of them. But hey, his loss is my gain!" Samantha said, tapping the palm of her hand against her chest. "Thanks to him we're getting to have some quality girlfriend time!"

"Yes, you're right," Julie said, unveiling her first full smile of the evening.

After they paid the check, Julie and Samantha left the restaurant and walked to the parking lot.

"Thanks for being my 'dame in shining armor' tonight," Julie said. She gave Samantha a goodbye hug.

"That's what friends are for," Samantha replied as she withdrew from their embrace. "And remember, don't call him!"

When Julie got back to her apartment, she headed straight to the living room, dropped her purse and jacket on the couch, and flopped down next to them. She slid off her shoes and kicked her legs onto the couch. Then she reached over to the coffee table, picked up the remote, and turned on the TV.

Julie clicked aimlessly. None of the shows caught her interest. She was well into her second lap through the cable channels when her cell phone rang. Julie grabbed her purse and pulled it out. Steve.

She tossed the phone onto the couch and went back to clicking the remote, finally settling on a rerun of *Law & Order: Special Victims Unit*. The phone rang again. She let it go to voice mail. It rang again. She didn't pick up.

I wish he would leave me alone! She tried to focus on the TV program. It rang again and again and again. The tenth time he called, Julie answered.

"Hi. Why are you calling?" she asked sternly.

"I'm calling to say I am sorry."

"Is the reason you're sorry because my friend yelled at you?"

"Yes, she gave me an earful. But I'm sorry either way. Let me make it up to you. Let me take you out again." Steve laughed nervously.

"Again? Hah! You're kidding, right?" she replied. "No, thanks. I'm not interested."

Julie hung up the phone and set the ringer to mute. Then she tossed it in her purse and went back to watching TV.

The Rest of the Story

Julie took a break from dating during the year that followed her non-night out with Steve. She deemed it her "men-free year." During those twelve months, she spent time hanging out with her girlfriends, her sister, and her four nieces and nephews.

Julie eased back into the dating scene the following year. She tried Match.com and eHarmony but didn't meet any men who she connected with especially well. Then she had an idea: Most of her friends were married with kids, and the same was true of their circles of friends. Why not help them out if they could help her out? Julie's "Babysitting for Boyfriends" program was born.

Julie created flyers. She distributed them to married friends with kids and asked that they share the flyers with people they knew. For every man she was introduced to and met in person, she'd provide one night of free babysitting as a thank-you to the parents who'd done the matchmaking.

Julie went on five first dates. The fifth man she went out with became her husband.

Dating Takeaway Tips

DON'T BE ASHAMED.

When Steve stood Julie up, she felt ashamed and humiliated. But it wasn't Julie who should have felt that way. She did *nothing* wrong. The two of them had made a plan. She stuck to it. He was the one who chose not to go to the restaurant, and not to contact her. Of the two of them, Steve should have been the one who felt embarrassed. His no-showing didn't reflect on Julie, as she feared it did. It showed that he was a thoughtless person. If something similar should ever happen to you, eat and drink with pride, hold your head high, and treat it like a date with your amazing self. It's not about you. It's about him.

MAKE THE MOST OF A DISAPPOINTMENT.

You know the saying, "When life gives you lemons, make lemonade." (Or you could add vodka!) Let that expression be your inspiration if the person you were supposed to go out with doesn't show up. You don't have to abandon your evening plans. Contact a friend or family member instead. Have them meet you wherever you are. The best antidote to a bad date, or a no-show, is quality time with a girlfriend, a BFF, a family member, or someone else who cares about you. Hang out with them. If they are too far away, talk or text through what happened. Share how you're feeling. Vent. Laugh. Complain. Even shed a tear or two. Get it out. Celebrate that you're using your valuable time to connect with a person who has your back instead of wasting it with someone who didn't come through for you.

Also, realize that the disappointment is actually a gift. This person has shown you their cards *early*. You may have dodged a bullet! Remember, dating offers the opportunity to learn about other people before you commit to anyone, and the more you find out straightaway, the better.

"Friendship is the inexpressible comfort of feeling safe with a person, having neither to weigh thoughts nor measure words."

— *George Eliot*
author and poet

The Two-in-One Date

A Match.com e-mail arrived in Monica's inbox one Wednesday morning in October: "*I like your picture and what's in your profile. Interested in meeting? – Joe.*" Monica clicked on a link that took her to Joe's profile. Her eyes were immediately drawn to the video in the middle of the page. Intrigued, she pressed on the "play" arrow and watched a man with brown hair, wearing a black T-shirt and jeans, doing a comedy set on stage at a nightclub.

He looked at ease delivering his set about the challenges of growing up in a traditional Italian family. Joe didn't berate people in the audience as comedians often do. The crowd laughed at his jokes. Monica did too. She liked his voice, his demeanor. His whole look was appealing to her. He seemed normal.

Monica had been in a series of long-term relationships through her twenties and thirties. The last one ended when she broke off her engagement with her boyfriend of two years. It had been difficult and painful, but she realized she couldn't marry a man for whom her love went no further than that of a deep friendship. It took her a year to start dating again. When she did, Monica decided she'd take a nonjudgmental approach. If a guy was interested in her, she'd give him the benefit of the doubt and go on a date with him. What followed were a lot of one-and-done dates with men who she discovered had too many quirks for her liking, intermixed with a few she wanted to get to know better.

Ten years of active dating passed. Monica longed to meet someone whose sensibilities, passions, and life views complemented her own. She e-mailed Joe back right away. *Yes, I'm interested in meeting. Call me.* Monica typed her office and cell numbers and hit "send."

She was busy at work in her office two days later when the phone rang.

"Hi, this is Joe," said the man on the other end of the line. She didn't recognize his voice. Nor could she think of any clients or colleagues who were named Joe. There was only one person it could be.

"My Joe?" she asked. There was silence on the other end of the line. Monica's face flushed. She winced. *I hope I didn't scare him off.*

"Ah . . . yes, this is Joe from online," the voice said cautiously.

"Thanks for calling me, Joe from online," she replied in a jovial tone, hoping to overcome the awkward start to the conversation. He laughed. Monica let out a quiet sigh of relief. "How are you doing today?"

"I'm good, thanks," he said. "And depending on how you answer this question, I may even be doing better. Would you like to meet for coffee tomorrow morning?"

Monica made a small fist-bump motion upward. "That sounds great. I'd like that very much."

After their meeting plans were set, Monica hung up the

phone and launched a full-fledged fist bump into the air. "Yes!" she called out. Then she sat down, surveyed the papers strewn across her desk, and got back to work.

Monica typically walked from her home to the bakery where she and Joe were meeting. But she was running late that Saturday morning and decided to drive. To avoid the inconvenience of feeding a meter, Monica parked in her church's almost empty lot a few blocks away. After getting out and locking her car, Monica inserted her earbuds and turned on her music. Looking around, she admired the beautiful day. The sky was a rich blue with intermittent clouds, and the leaves were turning from green to amber. There was a light, refreshing breeze.

Monica had opted to wear her Saturday morning uniform— a black Adidas-inspired sweat suit with a white stripe running down each side and white tennis shoes. To passersby, she'd easily be mistaken for a woman heading to the gym.

Better Joe see the everyday me right away, she reasoned.

As Monica walked the last of the residential blocks before crossing onto State Street, she turned her music off but kept her earbuds in. From a block away she saw Joe seated on a bench in front of the bakery. His clothes were almost identical to what he'd worn in the video, except his T-shirt was white.

Holy cow! He's cute! She picked up her pace.

As though he'd heard her thoughts, Joe turned to her, smiled, stood up, and waved. His smile was infectious, and Monica immediately smiled back.

They embraced in a brief, friendly hug. "Hi, Joe, I'm Monica," she said as she stepped back.

"It's really nice to meet you," he replied, looking straight into her eyes.

Joe was one or two inches shorter than Monica. She preferred to neither tower over nor be much shorter than her dates. Given that she rarely wore heels, Joe's height suited her well.

"Thanks for coming to get some coffee with me today. What are you listening to?" he asked. Monica had forgotten that white cords were still dangling from her ears. She quickly removed her earbuds and shoved them into her purse's outside pocket.

"I was listening to Kristin Chenoweth," she replied. "I loved her in *Wicked,* and a friend turned me on to her more spiritual music. But you probably don't listen to that type of music."

"Actually, I don't mind it," he replied. "But what I'm a really big fan of are bands from the seventies and eighties. I realize that I'm sounding super retro, but oh well. My favorite band is Styx."

"I sort of know their music," Monica said. "I think my brothers liked them. Honestly, I'm not much of a rocker. But I'm open to learning more!"

"That's great to know," Joe said. His smile returned. Tilting his head in the direction of the bakery, he asked, "How about we go inside and get that coffee I promised you?"

Joe held the bakery door open for her, allowing the scent of freshly baked bread to escape out to the street. Monica headed straight for the bakery counter and began perusing the treats in the display cases. They were filled with tortes, éclairs, petits fours, and other European desserts. Meanwhile, Joe was ordering their hot beverages.

"Would you like to get something with your coffee?" Joe asked. "And it's on me."

"That's very nice. Thanks," Monica replied. "Just coffee is fine. I had a big breakfast."

I'm liking his gentlemanly manners, and he's so handsome!

She took a seat at a table while Joe waited for the two cups to be poured. He brought them over and sat down. Their conversation started immediately and continued steadily for an hour. Monica shared what it was like being the sixth of nine children growing up in a Southern California city in the 1970s and '80s. Joe told her about the small town in Illinois that he came from where almost everyone knew each other.

"Looking back, I'm glad I was raised in a small town," he said. "But as I got older it shrunk from small to tiny. It became suffocating. That must be what happens when you have fifteen cousins living in the same community. I had to leave, so I moved to Springfield to go to the University of Illinois and never moved back. But I do return at least every two years for family reunions."

He took a sip of coffee. "Enough about me. What do you do for a living?"

Monica told him about her job as a customer relationship executive at a large management consulting firm. "A big part of my job is business development and expanding client relationships. I especially like leading training sessions with clients. Teaching comes naturally for me."

"That's a great skill to have. My job as an airplane mechanic is very different from yours," Joe said. "I get up at four a.m., before the sun rises. It's peaceful that early. And I never have to deal with traffic when I drive to the airport." Joe drank the last of his coffee. "I spend most of my workday around the roar of airplane engines. Of course, I have headphones on, but how's that for two extremes? My shift is over at three, so, unlike most people, when I get off work, I have plenty of daytime left to do other things. Maybe another time I'll tell you about the different businesses I have going on."

"That sounds so interesting," Monica said, gently sliding her empty coffee cup on the table between her hands.

Joe looked into his cup and then at Monica's. "How about we go for a walk? Did you drive? If you did, I can walk you to your car."

"Yes, I drove to my church's parking lot and headed over here," Monica said.

As they left the shop, their conversation quickly resumed. They discussed being raised Catholic and the important role that religion holds in each of their lives. They also discovered that they shared a passion for yoga.

"I kept going back after my neighbor took me to my first class," Monica said. "One day, years ago, the instructor didn't show up. None of us wanted it to be cancelled, so I volunteered to lead the class. It went great. I got tons of positive feedback. The recreation center hired me as a substitute instructor! Now that I'm certified, I teach my own class twice a week."

As Monica described why she named her class "Joy Yoga," Joe gently took her hand and put it in his. She looked down, smiled, and thrust their locked hands upward toward the sky. "Yahoo!" she called out. They laughed and continued strolling.

I am so happy to be out with a normal guy!

After detouring around the block twice, they arrived at the church's parking lot and stopped alongside Monica's driver's-side door. She was oblivious to the voices of people going by and the rumble of the passing cars' motors. Her attention was fully on Joe.

"Thanks for the coffee. I had a great time," Monica said.

"Me too," said Joe. "I hope I'm not too forward, but what are you doing tonight?"

"Nothing, actually," Monica said.

"Can I take you to dinner?"

"Yes! You sure can. I'd like that."

"Great. I'll pick you up at six."

Monica gave him her address, and they exchanged a brief hug before saying their goodbyes. As she drove her car out of the lot, Monica looked back to see Joe standing where she'd left him, watching her drive away.

⸺ ❧ ⸺

Monica completed her weekend errands faster than usual. When she returned home, she forced herself to do some ironing and clean the bathroom, her least favorite chores. Then she kicked back on the couch and munched on grapes she'd just bought at the store.

He seems like a great guy, but I wonder if I'm a good long-term match for an airplane mechanic? Monica rolled her eyes to herself. *Shame on me. I need to focus on the things that matter, like finding out who he is and how he treats others.*

She made sure to give herself enough time to get ready for her evening. After trying on several outfits, Monica opted to wear a black sweater with black pants. Her mom had once told her that everyone looks good in black. Over the years, Monica had transformed that adage into her fashion motto. When special occasions arose, black clothing was her go-to attire.

Her doorbell rang at exactly six o'clock. She opened the door to see Joe standing before her dressed in khaki pants and a blue button-up shirt.

"Hi! Great to see you again. You look very handsome," Monica said.

"Thanks. That's nice of you." Joe's cheeks turned slightly rosy. "You look great too."

Monica thanked Joe, picked up her black clutch from the entry hall table, and locked the door behind them. They traversed the stone path across the front yard to the sidewalk and his awaiting car. He opened the door for her, and she settled into the passenger seat. Joe got into the driver's seat, turned on the engine, and pulled onto the street. Fleetwood Mac's "Don't Stop" came on the radio.

"I hope you like Italian food," he said as they drove across an intersection, "because I'm taking you to my favorite Italian restaurant, Ristorante Francesco."

"Of course I like Italian food," Monica responded. "Pastas, the yummy sauces, prosciutto and melon, tiramisu, the wines . . . What's not to like?"

"That's good to hear because I own a pasta sauce business," Joe said, momentarily taking his eyes off the road to see Monica's response.

"You do? You're a mechanic *and* a sauce maker? That's a first for me!"

Joe spent the rest of the drive telling her about his sauce company. "Yeah, it's one of my side businesses. I love to cook. People were regularly telling me how fresh and flavorful my pasta sauce was. They kept wanting to take some home with them. So, one day I thought, why not make it, bottle it, and sell it?"

"That's so cool," Monica said. "Where did you get the recipe from?"

"My sauce is based on my mom's recipe. She's the one who got me into cooking. My sister, brother, and I all love her food. Well, the entire family does. The three of us decided that her recipes needed to be freed from the green index card box that she had jammed all her old recipes into. We wanted to share them with people who appreciate good Italian food. It was a big project. We eventually published a cookbook."

"No way! Are they both for sale somewhere?" Monica asked. "Can I buy the book and your sauce?"

"The cookbook is on Amazon. For years my mom was also selling it out of the trunk of her car. My sauce is sold at Whole Foods and a few other grocery stores. If we keep getting to know each other better, I'll be happy to give you a copy of the book and a bottle or two of the sauce." Joe winked and then paused. He looked over at her again. "Hey, am I sounding like a game show host? Get to know me, and you, the lucky winner, will get some fabulous prizes!" They laughed.

Monica relaxed into the passenger seat and reached into her purse for a tissue. As she wiped the tears that Joe's joke had spawned, she realized how foolish she'd been to question whether his being a mechanic would make them incompatible.

Joe found a parking space a block from the restaurant.

Monica got out of his Acura and watched from the sidewalk as Joe opened the trunk and pulled out a small black bag. She gasped.

Whoa! He carries a clutch? I don't know any guys who do that.

Joe joined her on the sidewalk. The bag was in his right hand. Monica glanced inconspicuously at the purse as they walked. It was about eight inches wide and five inches high, with a red-and-black Tumi label stitched near the top seam. Joe seemed at ease with the accessory.

When they stepped into Ristorante Francesco, Monica's focus shifted from Joe's clutch to the restaurant. The back wall was jam-packed with stacked bottles. Bunches of plastic grapes were tacked up haphazardly around the shelving. Two Baroque, five-foot-tall paintings of medieval peasants cheerfully holding cherubs and grapes sat directly across from the entrance. The paintings were encased in ornate gold leaf frames.

The hostess led them to a table in front of the street-facing window. On the wall to Monica's left was a photo collage of celebratory diners from years past whose luster had succumbed to the sun's daily gaze.

Joe handed Monica one of the two menus the hostess had left on the table. "The homemade pasta they serve here is very fresh tasting. They make a new batch every day. I always order the pasta special, and I've never regretted it."

A busboy placed a bread basket on the table. They each helped themselves to a slice of the warm baguette. Monica perused the menu while Joe munched on the bread and studied the map of Italian wine regions that lay sandwiched between the white tablecloth and glass tabletop.

It was Monica's practice to order pasta when she was on a dinner date for the first time with a guy. Pasta dishes were usually less expensive than meat and fish entrées. Upon the waiter's return, they ordered two glasses of Chianti, two Caesar salads, one pasta special, the pasta primavera, and dessert.

As soon as the waiter left with their orders, Monica gave in to her curiosity. "I can't hold off any longer. What's with the bro bag?"

Joe looked confused. Monica pointed at the Tumi bag that he'd placed beside him on the tabletop.

"Oh, this?" Joe asked, pointing to his clutch. "Sorry, I've never heard the term 'bro bag' before. What, you don't like my bag? It's so metro."

"What do you mean by 'metro'?" Monica asked.

"You know, metrosexual."

"Metrosexual? You're a metrosexual? I've never heard that word before."

Joe's eyebrows raised slightly. "You haven't? You must have. You know, straight guys who live in urban areas and go the extra distance to take care of themselves. We don't buy crappy grooming products. We'll spend a little extra on shampoos and conditioners. We exercise regularly. Many metrosexuals will only buy finely made clothes, but that part's not exactly me." Joe chuckled. "You probably know other guys who fit this description."

"I do, but none of them have told me that they're metrosexuals, and none of them carry a purse. What do you have in there?" Monica leaned forward, trying to peer into Joe's bag.

Joe unzipped it and looked inside. "Things. My wallet, a comb, my phone, my asthma inhaler."

"Hmmm . . . Can't you carry those things elsewhere? Your back pocket, your jacket pocket, in the car?"

Joe zippered the clutch and looked at Monica. "I don't think you like my bag, do you?"

"I don't," Monica said, smiling. "I have nothing against you being a metrosexual. But I'm just not used to a guy carrying a bag. I think you're sexier without the purse."

Joe threw his head back and burst out laughing. His laughter was so infectious, Monica couldn't help but giggle.

"Can we agree that only one of us should carry a black clutch, and that person should be me?" she asked after their laughter subsided.

Joe placed the bag on the floor beside him. "All right, it's gone for now. I've got to say, you sure put it out there, don't you?"

"Yes, that's me. Everything on my mind comes right out of my mouth. Well, not always, but most of the time." Monica stared up at the ceiling for a few seconds. Joe watched as she refocused back on him. "I realize that I can go a bit too far sometimes. I'm working on it. I didn't mean to offend you."

"No, you didn't offend me. I find your honesty refreshing," he replied.

Her smile reemerged. "How about we change topics? When you were telling me about your sauce business you said that it was only one of your side businesses. You have others?"

"Remember how I told you I love to cook?" Joe asked. "My second business also has to do with food. It's called 'Girls Dine In.' It's a comedy cooking party company."

Monica burst out laughing. "Comedy cooking parties for women? Do you do that to meet single ladies?"

"Uh . . . actually, yes. At least, that's how it started out," Joe said as Monica's laughter died down. "It's not so easy for us guys in our forties to meet nice single women. I've taught cooking classes at Sur La Table and other stores. So I figured, why not start my own home cooking school for women? And I could differentiate my business by weaving in material from my comedy routine. It seemed like a good idea."

"I've got to hand it to you," she said as she dabbed laughter-induced tears from the corners of her eyes with her napkin. "You're a creative guy."

"You could say that I'm a creative cooker. To get the business going I advertised on Craigslist and other places. Female clients have hired me. But things didn't work out as I had expected. Most of the time the women invited their boyfriends, and the dinners turned into couples' cooking parties." Joe stopped speaking as their salads were being served. "No dates came out of it," he said after the waiter left. "Not one. That was okay. I had fun teaching people how to make meals. But prepping for those parties got to be way too much work."

Over their first and second courses, Joe and Monica talked about his cooking class company and how Joe came to do comedy through a self-improvement seminar he took. They discovered that they both were readers of self-help books and believed in the importance of being true to their inner selves.

"I want you to know that I'm having a good time tonight," Monica said as soon as the waiter left with their empty dinner plates.

"Me too!" Joe replied, smiling. "I had a feeling that I would. Maybe this is a good time to tell you something. I'm probably jumping ahead too fast, but I think I should share something that may, or may not, make a difference to you."

Joe looked down at his napkin. Monica watched as he took a deep breath and set his gaze back on her.

"Sure, what is it?" Monica asked hesitantly.

"You need to know that I don't want to have kids."

Monica leaned back in her chair. *I'm amazed we have so much in common.* After a few moments, she sat forward again. "Actually, I don't either."

"You don't?"

Monica shook her head.

"Understandably, many women do," he said. "When I start dating a woman I like, I tell her this right away. That's why I felt I had to mention it to you."

"Having kids was one of the main issues with my ex-fiancé," Monica said. "He wanted them, and I didn't. With eight brothers and sisters, I'm Aunt Monica to fifteen nieces and nephews! That's a lot of kids to help raise. I'm not lacking for time with children, and I love being with them. It's great to have an impact on their lives."

Noticing that the hum of voices around them had gotten louder, Monica scanned the room and saw that all the tables in the small restaurant had been filled. She leaned forward, her body pressing gently against the tabletop.

"The way I see it, there are too many kids in this world who don't get enough, or maybe any, guidance, support, or love from adults. Instead of bringing more children into the world, I feel that my calling is to help the ones in need who have already been born."

Joe nodded. "I completely agree with you."

"Also, let's be honest," she said. "There's a certain freedom that people have when they're not rearing children. And there's usually less stress. No babysitters, no car pools, no endless crying and time-outs. People who don't have kids can pretty much do what they want, when they want. Their schedules are their own. That's the lifestyle that works best for me."

"And for me too," Joe said. "I had no idea how you'd respond to my talking about kids already. I'm glad I mentioned it, and I'm really glad we share the same view."

The waiter approached with the tiramisu Monica had ordered in one hand and the cannoli for Joe in the other. While she watched the dishes and flatware being placed onto the table, Monica noticed out of the corner of her eye that Joe was oblivious to the commotion happening in front of them. He was looking straight at her.

This is a man I could see myself with. But I want to do this right. I don't want to rush things.

They delved into their desserts. Joe offered Monica a taste of his cannoli, which she gladly accepted. He tried her tiramisu.

After finishing off the last bite, Monica blotted her upper lip to remove any crème that had escaped her fork and returned her napkin to her lap.

"Joe, now it's my turn to say something that might be jumping ahead too quickly. I really like you, and I have a feeling we could have a great time together. Did you ever see the movie *The 40-Year-Old Virgin?* Steve Carell starred in it. Like they did in that movie, I think we should wait twenty-eight dates before we have sex."

Joe almost choked on the piece of cannoli in his mouth. He lunged forward as it slid out and back onto the dessert plate. Joe looked down at the rejected remnant and then broke out in laughter.

"Monica, I had a feeling that getting to know you would be a different experience than any other woman I've met." Joe shook his head. "But I had no idea that this deal you're proposing would be one of the reasons. Why would you want us to hold off for so long?"

"It's because I think you're a special guy. You're different from most men I've met—in a good way. If things work out between us, I promise you I'll fuck your brains out. But before I do that, I want us to get to know each other well so that when it does happen, it has meaning."

Joe shook his head again. "Tell you what, how about I think about your idea and we can talk about it another time?"

"Okay, that's fair. That's fine with me."

The brief silence that descended upon them was interrupted by the waiter, who arrived with the check. After Joe paid for the meal, they got up and started toward the exit. To Monica's surprise, Joe stopped a waitress who was walking by.

"Would you mind taking our photo?" he asked, handing his cell phone to her before she could respond.

The waitress agreed and had Monica and Joe pose near the entrance. As they readied themselves for the photo, Joe tucked the purse he held in his right hand behind his back. He then gently placed his arm around Monica, his left hand lightly touching her left shoulder. Feeling his arm against her jacket, Monica's already radiant smile beamed even brighter. "Cheese!" they said in unison.

Joe recognized Francesco, the owner and restaurant's name-sake, standing a few yards away. He waved the older man over to join them in a second photo. "The meal was wonderful," Joe told Francesco after their photo had been taken. "Your food is always delicious." He introduced Monica. The three of them talked briefly about her love of Italy and Italian food and then said, "Arrivederci!"

During the drive to Monica's home, Joe confessed that earlier that afternoon he'd driven by her place. "I wanted to make sure that I wasn't late to pick you up. I figured that if I drove to and from your house, I'd know how to get there and how long the drive would take."

Monica touched his arm. "I'm so flattered that you took time out of your Saturday afternoon to do that. You're a good guy, Joe," she said, and then removed her hand.

When they arrived at Monica's house, Joe parked his car and turned off the engine. "I had a really good time tonight, Monica. I'd like to see you again."

Monica smiled. "I'm happy that you do. I'd like that too."

She felt her heartbeat accelerate, and a gentle magnetic force took hold. Monica's eyelids closed as she gradually leaned toward Joe. Their lips met in a tender goodnight kiss. Withdrawing, Monica opened her eyes to see Joe's remain closed for a few more seconds.

"I've had a great two-in-one first date with you, Joe. Thanks very much. I look forward to whatever's coming next."

Monica picked up her purse from where it rested on the floor mat. She opened the door, stepped onto the sidewalk, and closed the door behind her. Monica glided up the pathway to her front door. Upon unlocking it, she turned around, blew a kiss to Joe, and went inside.

The Rest of the Story

Joe agreed to Monica's twenty-eight-date plan. During that time period, not a day went by when they didn't see one another, whether it was for a brief hello or a more traditional date. When date twenty-eight arrived, Monica made good on her promise!

Six months after they met, they began partially living together, or as Joe says jokingly, "I infiltrated her life." On the one-year anniversary of their first date, Joe took Monica back to Ristorante Francesco for dinner. Unbeknownst to her, he'd had the photo they'd taken there twelve months earlier framed, requested the same table as before, and had driven to the restaurant a day earlier to drop off the portrait. It awaited them on the table when they were seated. Monica loved the surprise!

Joe proposed five years later. He had wanted to ask Monica to marry him years earlier, but she was unsure if she wanted to get married, although she *was* sure she wanted to spend her life with Joe. After half a decade as a couple, she evolved her thinking and enthusiastically replied, "Yes!" They became husband and wife seven years after their first date. The couple still lives in the house where Joe picked Monica up for the second part of their two-in-one date.

In the back of one of their closets sits the bro bag, gathering dust.

Dating Takeaway Tips

DON'T JUDGE OR JUMP TO CONCLUSIONS.

You could unintentionally take a promising meeting and sabotage it. Don't assume anything about anyone, even if you've scoured the Internet for your date's backstory before the two of you meet. The whole point of going on a date is to get to know a new person. Let them be the one to tell you about themselves. Grant them the time and space. Ask them questions in a friendly, casual manner. No one wants to be subject to an inquisition. Build a portrait of them in your mind based on what they tell you, what you observe, and what you experience together.

Don't assume an attitude that you are superior to the person you're meeting. The playing field should be level. Judgments are rooted in self-righteousness and an "I'm right and you're wrong" mentality. Evaluate instead. If you tend to be critical of people, suspend that trait. Hold back criticizing what your date is telling you and doing (unless it's blatantly offensive). Instead, take it all in. Have an open mind. It's the character and the quality of the individual that matters, not the job title, income level, or pedigree. They may turn out to be a far more interesting, fun, and kind person than you'd ever imagined.

YOU'RE AN ADULT. HAVE ADULT CONVERSATION.

Talking about your favorite movies and where you like to vacation is okay for the first moments of a first date, but it doesn't tell you anything of actual value about a person. If you're dating to find love, don't be afraid to get to the "real stuff," and don't hold back when you are interested!

Monica and Joe put so much out there on their first date! They talked about whether they wanted kids, when they should have sex, failed businesses, even the fact that she didn't like his clutch! He discussed his family and how they influenced his businesses. They freely exchanged compliments. Most importantly, they each shared how much they enjoyed being together and were crystal clear about wanting to keep learning more.

"The very first moment I beheld him,
my heart was irrevocably gone."

— *Jane Austen*
author

The Cringe

Maria sent the first e-mail. Like so many other nights, she'd been clicking her way through an endless stream of photos of middle-aged men with graying, receding, or departed hair when she spotted him. Something about Pup-Man232's smile stood out. There was a sweetness to it. He had a full head of brown hair and looked trim, like a guy who visits the gym weekly.

His Match.com profile held more promise than most. Pup-Man worked in real estate. So did she. He was an economist. She was attracted to smart men. He loved dogs. She liked them but had never owned one. He had worked in Eastern Europe during the 1980s. Traveling internationally was a passion of hers. He had posted a photo of himself standing on the Great Wall of China wearing a T-shirt from Zingerman's, her college town's most popular deli. During her senior year at the University of Michigan, she had worked at Zingerman's. And by chance, just a week earlier, Maria's college friend had sent her a T-shirt with the deli's logo emblazoned on it.

Maybe he's also a Michigan alum? Even if he wasn't, they'd have enough in common to make for a pleasant first date. Maria began typing.

It may seem a bit cliché, but I like what I read in your profile. I'm intrigued. Check out mine, and if you want to be in touch, you know how to find me. Best, Maria.

She clicked "Send."

The e-mail PupMan—whose real name was Adam—sent her thirty minutes later was short but friendly.

Hi. I like your profile too. I could be the "curious, candid, and caring guy" you wrote about wanting to meet. There's a photo of you hiking. Nice! Where are some of your favorite places to go on a day hike?

She replied with a few more details about herself before going to bed. His next e-mail arrived the following morning.

I think it's great that you're in real estate too. I started out as an economist researching and writing papers few people read. Now I'm an urban planner, but don't blame me for the problems in this city! Happy to take credit for the stuff that works, though.

In his third e-mail, he made his move.

Would you like to meet on Sunday afternoon? We could take a walk around the lake. It's supposed to be a nice day.

Maria e-mailed back right away to accept, and after exchanging a few logistical messages, their date was on.

He'll probably be 50 percent of what I'm expecting, Maria thought as she pulled her Honda Accord into the lakeside parking lot. Decades of dating experience had taught her to temper her expectations before every first date.

I really hope this isn't a waste of a perfectly good afternoon. I broke my every-other-day hair-washing schedule for this guy!

She got out of the car and headed toward the park bench where Adam had suggested they meet. From halfway across the parking lot, she could see a man who looked to be around five foot ten, the height that Adam had listed in his profile. But he had a bulging belly, which the man in the photos had not. As Maria got closer, she saw that his beard—another surprise—and hair were heavier on the salt, and lighter on the pepper, than the pictures had foretold.

Ugh! Yet another guy who's twenty to thirty pounds heavier, and five to ten years older, than his photos. Grrr! I'm already here, so I'll suck it up and try not to be distracted by his stomach. Maybe his personality will make up for the false advertising.

"You must be Adam," Maria said when she was within a few feet of him.

"That's me," he replied jovially. They hugged in an awkward we-don't-know-each-other-but-we-should-hug-as-though-we-do sort of way, their chests remaining a few inches apart.

"You're right on time," Adam said, stepping back from the hug. "That's great! I like it when people are punctual. How about we start walking?"

And so began their hour stroll around the lake. Their casual strides were in sync as they launched into conversation. Adam talked about his love for Riley, his golden retriever who was always seated on the entrance hall mat when he returned home from work.

"She's my biggest admirer," Adam said, and chuckled. "Nice to have a woman at home who appreciates me so."

Maria laughed. "Your screen name, PupMan232, was a dead giveaway that you like dogs. I didn't grow up with any, and all my apartments have been too small to keep one. But I've always liked them. I sometimes spend time with my friend and her German pinscher at their neighborhood dog park."

"I get it," Adam responded. "As much as I love Riley, she does make it hard to be spontaneous. Traveling is one of my greatest passions, but because of her I can't just decide on a whim to go somewhere."

"I like to travel too," Maria said as she pulled her brown North Face fleece vest out of her bag and put it on. The temperature had started to drop, though that didn't seem to bother the three teenage boys they'd just passed launching a wooden rowboat into the lake.

"I haven't been to China yet, but clearly you have," she said. "That was a neat photo of you standing on the Great Wall of China wearing your Zingerman's shirt. I worked there in college. Did you go to the University of Michigan too?"

"No, I didn't. I just ate at the deli when I was in Ann Arbor a few years ago. Their Reuben sandwich was the best I've ever had, so I had to have their T-shirt. I've worn it all over the world —India, Brazil, Argentina."

Adam shared stories from his international travels and then veered to the career topic. Maria told him she was a real estate

broker with five agents in her office, and Adam explained what
he did as an urban planner.

"It's my job to figure out how to make major cities more liv-
able, for more people, and still keep the energy usage and carbon
footprint down. My firm works with high-density housing de-
velopers."

"Ah-ha! So, *you're* the one behind all the new high-rise
buildings going up and all the crazy roadwork that's happening
around them," Maria said.

"Well, sort of. There's a lot of good that comes from increas-
ing the housing supply." Adam paused. "What can I say? I enjoy
what I do and am passionate about it. I like to think of myself as
more of the solution than the problem."

The conversation transitioned to Adam's divorce as they
walked around the far end of the lake.

"Thinking back on it now, I never should have made a lifelong commitment when I was only twenty-two," he said.

Maria looked over at him. "Twenty-two? Wow, that is
young. Did you two just grow apart?"

"Yeah, we were very different people back then, just living in
the moment. The only long-view topic we discussed was not
having children. But really, I just wasn't mature enough back
then to know who I was going to turn out to be twenty or thirty
years later."

"In some ways, I think I've benefited by not getting married when so many of my friends did," Maria said. "Now that
I'm in my fifties, I absolutely know who I am and where I'm
headed." She smiled. Some of those friends were still happily
married. Others only saw the men they had promised their

lives to because of the co-parenting terms in their custody agreements.

"Most of my newly single girlfriends are back in the dating scene, trying to figure it all out," she said. "And then there's me. I'm a pro at dating because I've never left it." Maria laughed but wondered if she was disclosing more about her singlehood than she should on a first date.

"I can tell you've got a healthy attitude about life. You seem pretty at ease about sharing what you're thinking," Adam said.

Maria glanced at him. He returned her gaze without breaking his stride, his brown eyes glowing with kindness.

"I appreciate that in a woman," he added.

"Thanks for telling me that," Maria said. She looked over at the lake and saw two twenty-something girls paddling a silver canoe. The sun's rays glistened on the water and reflected off their tarnished aluminum boat.

"Like everyone, I've had my share of challenges," she continued. "How can you not at this point?"

"What's one of your challenges?" he asked, sounding like he genuinely wanted to know.

"Thyroid cancer," she answered. "I overcame it, but after I was diagnosed, I resolved that I would no longer keep things locked inside. Suppressing my emotions was unhealthy. I decided to tell things as I saw them. I'd be honest with people but not go overboard to the point of being rude. There are limits. You'd think as a native New Yorker, it would be natural for me." She laughed. "My mom is the one in the family who tells things as she sees them. My dad was more reserved. I used to take after him in that area, but not anymore."

"How awful that you had cancer. It must have been a really hard and scary time. But you seem to be doing incredibly well now. You're running a business; you're leading a busy and exciting life."

"You're right. Life is good," Maria said. "I would never wish what I went through on anybody. But it is great to be on the other side of it and living my life."

"I'm pleased to hear that," Adam said. "By the way, I don't think you've told me your last name. What is it?"

"It's Ayala. Why do you ask?"

"Just wondering," Adam said, his voice trailing off as he looked across the lake at the three boys in the rowboat. They were slapping the water with their oars, splashing each other. A startled flock of birds resting on a nearby rock lifted into the air and flew off.

As the paint-chipped bench where Maria and Adam had begun their walk came into view, Maria realized she didn't want their conversation to end just yet.

Okay, Adam's beard, flat nose, and build remind me of my grandpa Luis, but he's also smart and super engaging like Grandpa was. Too bad Adam's not in better shape, but the guy is sweet, and that's a rare quality in the men I meet these days. I could spend more time with him.

Adam walked to the bench and sat down. Instead of looking at Maria, who seated herself to his right, he directed his gaze downward and fixed it on his left shoe.

"Is everything all right?" she asked.

"Ah, sure," he said, still looking away.

They sat in silence, Maria's hands folded in her lap, the lakeside breeze gently tossing her curly hair and rustling the tree leaves behind them. Her heartbeat escalated as she waited for Adam to say something, anything.

What's going on?

After a minute or two, Adam turned to Maria. "I need to tell you something." The levity in his voice had evaporated. Maria braced herself.

"What? Just tell me. Whatever it is, it's fine," she replied, with a mix of warmth and exasperation in her voice.

"This is not the first time we've met. We've been out on a date before. Maybe you remember? We had lunch at a French restaurant downtown fourteen years ago."

Maria stared at him in disbelief. She scoured her memory, desperately waiting—hoping—for a recollection of their prior date to emerge. Even a faint reminiscence would provide her with needed clues. She was sure her synapses were firing, but no flashback appeared. Her memory was a wasteland. Her muscles tensed up. A cringe swept through her body.

"So much time has passed. I'm sure neither of us looks exactly as we did nearly a decade and a half ago. Are you *sure* it was me you went out with?" she asked after an extended pause.

Have I just spent all this time with a guy who I've already been out with? How come I can't remember him?

"When you told me you'd had cancer, it hit me. Years ago, I went out with a brunette woman. She was a real estate broker, like you. She had gone through thyroid cancer, like you. That's why I asked for your last name."

Maria sat silently.

"You probably don't remember this either then. At the end

of that date, I invited you out again," he continued. "Your answer was no. When I asked you why, you told me it was because you wanted to be with a guy who is more sensitive than I am."

Maria wanted to look away, to redirect her gaze to anywhere but his eyes. But she didn't. She felt the red crawling up her face. She wasn't sure which was worse: going on a second date nearly a decade and a half later with the same guy she'd rejected once already, or not remembering anything about meeting him the first time. But her embarrassment didn't matter. She needed to hear him out. It was the least she could do.

Adam leaned forward, his hands pressing down on the edge of the bench. "I don't know how you came up with that take on me," he said. "I'm not some guy who is all jacked up on testosterone. I have a soft side. For goodness sakes, I like cats!"

Maria managed to squelch her laugh before it burst out; the noise that escaped her lips sounded more like a hiccup.

"After you turned me down, I remember replaying the date in my mind. I tried to figure out where you got that misimpression of me. It may have been because I changed the topic when you started telling me about your thyroid cancer."

Maria wasn't sure what to say. She hoped it would come to her as she spoke. She inhaled, released slowly, and began.

"That may have been it," she said. "From what you've described, we probably met about a year after my treatment ended. It took me a while to realize that, back then, I was overly sensitive to how people responded to my illness. I'm sorry about that."

"The reason I changed the subject was because I didn't want to force you to dwell on your cancer," he said softly. "There has been cancer in my family, and I just didn't want to bring you down during our date. It wasn't avoidance. It was concern."

I feel horrible. Why can't I remember anything about that date?

"You know what? It was a long time ago," Maria said. "No need to dwell on what happened between us then. As far as I'm concerned, this is our first date."

"You're right. It was ages ago," Adam said. "How about we get together another time?"

"That would be lovely," she said. "One thing you can be sure about—I'll never forget *this* first date!"

The Rest of the Story

Maria and Adam went out on four more dates. Initially she was really excited to get to know him better. But by their fifth date, the conversation no longer flowed easily. It felt forced. She realized their connection had faded. Adam must have detected the change too. He didn't ask Maria out again, but she wasn't upset. She started dating someone else soon after. Months later, Adam e-mailed her to invite her to a real estate industry event. They are now friends who occasionally attend professional functions together. And Maria resolved to never again judge how a man handles difficult subjects that come up on a first date.

Dating Takeaway Tips

KEEP A JOURNAL.

To avoid what happened to Maria, it's wise to keep track of who you're engaging with on dating sites and apps, as well as any potential love interests you meet when you're out and about in the world. If you go on a dating binge, recording who you're in touch with will help you keep everything straight. Get yourself a paper journal, set up a spreadsheet, or create a list on your phone. It's helpful to capture each person's name, their dating site handle if the two of you connect online, and a few specific things you know about them. That way you won't accidentally talk to Bob about his two daughters in college when it was Bill who told you about his kids! If you're a seasoned dater, check your journal before you say yes to a date so that you avoid unintentionally going out with the same person twice.

BE NICE TO YOUR DATE.

We should always treat others as *we* want to be treated. Words have an impact. What you say to someone, and how you treat them, could very well remain with them for the rest of their days. That's what happened with Adam. Act kindly to the person you're out with, even if you decide you're not interested in them romantically or they aren't being as courteous as you'd like them to be. We're all human, and dating is inherently a vulnerable experience. Coming from a place of compassion for yourself and the people you meet, even if you find them annoying or outrageous, will always serve you well during your dating journey.

"Happiness is good health and a bad memory."

— *Ingrid Bergman*
actress

Dinner Al Fresco

ita glanced down at the bouquet of flowers in her hand as she followed the hostess past rows of empty tables and onto the café's rear patio. Even though both women were wearing masks, she was intent on keeping a distance of at least six feet between them until they'd stepped outside. Rita hadn't looked behind her to see whether Raj was trailing her by a similar distance.

Raj had been easy to recognize standing in front of the café. His salt-and-pepper hair and his brown eyes, which shone brightly against the navy-blue mask resting below them, were true to the photos Rita had viewed on Match.

After they said their hellos, Raj handed her a bouquet of rust-colored mums and pale orange lilies.

"Ah . . . thank you," she said. Rita wasn't used to being on the receiving end of such a grand first date gesture.

His first message, which he'd sent the previous Thursday, had also been kind and filled with flattery.

"I read your profile and you seem terrific. You touched my heart. Are you for real? Let's talk and get to know each other. I think we could be a great match. Btw, you are very pretty."

Rita was intrigued but wary of such an adoring opening volley. She opted for a tempered response but made sure to include a dash of flirtation.

"Thanks for your note and the compliment. How are you holding up during this crazy time? You don't believe that I'm real? Well, you're welcome to call me and find out."

Cell phone numbers were exchanged. Raj phoned her that night. They touched on an array of subjects during their twenty-minute call. A mutual love for dogs was discovered. Raj divulged that he had an ex-wife and two sons in their thirties. Rita mentioned that she'd never been married and didn't have any children. She shared that she'd recently ended a five-year relationship with a man whose inability to communicate openly and to fully express his feelings had doomed their future together.

When Rita and Raj talked about the steps they each were taking to avoid getting Covid-19, she determined that his level of caution was similar to hers. As the conversation wound down, Raj suggested they meet for dinner and offered to do the thirty-something-minute drive from Fort Lauderdale to her neighborhood in Miami.

"You pick the restaurant. We're living in a strange time. I want you to feel comfortable," he'd said.

Rita agreed and promised to get back to him with some options. Their date was set for Tuesday night.

Rita didn't know what to make of his parting request. The men she went out with usually selected the restaurant. This ritual had meaning to her. She viewed it as an early indicator of a take-charge personality, a quality she wanted in her future partner. Rita also took it as a sign that her date was interested in her.

Am I not even worthy of a few minutes of his time? Can't he just google some restaurants and pick one?

After calling a friend and talking through her concerns, Rita decided to put them aside. The next day, she texted Raj the names of two restaurants. Once he selected the café, she made a reservation for 7:00 p.m. and sent him the details.

Rita was more excited about the date after receiving Raj's text on Monday.

"Just 24 hours and 45 minutes. Do you think I'm looking forward to seeing you? Talk to you soon."

With decades of dating behind her, and the hard-fought perspective she'd accumulated over her fifty-five years, Rita usually wasn't overly optimistic when heading out on a first date. More often than not she was underwhelmed by the men she met. It wasn't that they needed to have a certain profession or earn a certain income. It was because she was clear about the qualities she wanted in a partner and didn't want to waste time with men who didn't appear to be right for her.

࿇

"Thank you for the beautiful flowers. I'm sorry again about being late," Rita said as she placed the bouquet and her small black handbag on the table before sitting down. "You got my text, didn't you?"

Raj nodded as he took his seat.

Rita's level of comfort increased after she scanned the patio and noticed that the occupied tables around them were more than six feet away. Without any discussion, they removed the straps from behind their ears in unison and put their masks away. In the months since Rita had gone from virtual dating back to in-person dating, she had been on five outdoor dinner dates. Each time, she and her date removed their masks after they were seated, and thankfully, she had remained virus-free.

"You look very pretty. I'm happy to see you," Raj said.

Rita smiled. She was glad she'd worn her black pencil skirt, long-sleeved red silk blouse and cropped black jacket. There was something about that outfit that made her feel sexy. Maybe he sensed it?

"Thank you. That's very nice of you. And you look really good too," she replied. Rita did think he was attractive. Not overly handsome, but attractive. She didn't mind that he'd paired sneakers with his black jeans. The look jived with his easygoing aura that Rita had first picked up on during their call.

After reviewing the menu, they settled on drinks and main courses, and then Raj suggested they share a starter. They decided on the shrimp ceviche, then quickly moved on to a discussion about their dogs. "Tell me about Rusty," Rita asked. "How old is he?"

Raj told her that the dog was a six-year-old rescue. "He's a really sweet chocolate Lab with tons of energy. We take regular hikes together. We also go to the dog park a few times a week. There's a poodle that Rusty enjoys playing with there. My hunch is that he has a crush on her. What about Breezy?"

"Breezy is super affectionate, which I think most Doodles are. He loves to cuddle on the couch. I'll be watching TV, and he'll lay his head on me here." Rita pointed to her midriff. "He's like my child."

"What a sweet boy," said Raj. "I'm sure our dogs would get along."

After the appetizer and drinks were served, the conversation shifted to careers.

"What do you like about being an interior designer?" Raj asked. "Given that I'm a real estate agent, I've been in a lot of homes that are poorly decorated. Makes me wonder about those owners. I bet you're good at what you do."

Rita finished placing a second spoonful on her plate before responding. "It's a rewarding challenge to take a space that isn't working for someone and give new life to it in a way that hopefully helps my clients live happily within it," Rita said. "You take the rest of the ceviche. This is more than enough for me."

"You're a special woman. I'm sure that your clients love working with you," Raj said, his smile shining brightly. Rita smiled warily in return.

The compliments keep coming. His love bombing is a bit overwhelming.

"How long have you been a real estate agent?" Rita asked as Raj began to eat. "The pandemic must have really shaken your business up. I hear people are moving out of tall buildings so they don't have to share elevators and run into neighbors unexpectedly."

"That's true," he said. "Single-family homes are more in demand than many condos, but I don't see that lasting. As you know, real estate is about cycles. I expect things will change back in time."

"So you're not worried? I remember you telling me on the phone that much of your business is selling condos."

"No, how can I be worried right now? I'm enjoying my time with you!"

They talked about the real estate markets in their two cities until the appetizer was finished and the plates were removed.

"You're an interesting woman. I can tell we're going to have fun together." Raj leaned forward and placed his hand on Rita's, which was resting on the table.

Her muscles tensed up, jolting her into a posture that would have made her childhood ballet teacher proud. Raj continued talking as if nothing had happened, while Rita's attention was transfixed on his warm, slightly clammy palm that was shielding her hand from the evening breeze.

What is he doing? I barely know this guy. He needs to slow down. And there's a pandemic going on. Why is he touching me without asking?

"Here's an idea," Raj continued. "We could take our dogs for a walk on the beach. Or maybe tennis? Do you play? I used to play a lot with my ex-wife. Obviously, that's over with. You and I should hit the ball around sometime."

"I haven't played tennis in years," Rita said, looking him in the eye. "I probably wouldn't be a very good tennis partner. As for the dog walking, we'll see. Breezy does love to run along the beach."

She slid her hand out from below his and reached for her teacup.

Over their main courses they spoke more about their careers, their upbringings, and places they'd like to travel to after the pandemic was over. At one point, the noise of some trucks driving by, combined with the exuberance of the diners around them, made it hard for Rita to hear what Raj had said.

"Are you wanting to go diving or flying in the Bahamas? Could you say that again? I didn't catch it."

"Wait. I had trouble hearing what you just said a minute ago! Is becoming hard of hearing the first activity we're doing together?" he said jokingly. They both laughed. "Actually, we're too young to be losing our hearing. Especially you!"

"I don't know about that," Rita replied, grinning. Raj only had four years on her, after all.

They both replied "yes" after the server asked whether they had enough room left for dessert. While perusing the menu, they discovered they shared a love of chocolate.

"Believe it or not, my favorite is M&M's. There so many high-end, fancy chocolate bars these days, and I prefer the same chocolate I ate as a kid," Rita said, chuckling.

They agreed to share a slice of chocolate cake and plunged their forks into it after the dessert was placed on the table.

"This is delicious," Rita said as she slid some of the remaining cake and raspberry coulis onto her fork.

"A sweet dessert for a sweet woman," Raj said before finishing the last piece. "I'm a man who says what he thinks. I really like you."

"Thank you. That's very nice of you. I've been having a good time getting to know you too."

He's definitely an ego booster, but this guy seems awfully anxious to be in a relationship.

Raj paid the bill without hesitancy. He signed the receipt, and they stood to gather their things. Rita reached into her purse, pulled out her mask, and was starting to strap it behind her ear when Raj suddenly leaned in and planted his moist lips on hers. She gasped.

OMG! He ambushed me in the middle of the café! We're in a pandemic! Does he know no boundaries? Maybe we don't share the same view of personal safety after all.

Raj was just standing there with the smile he'd worn for most of the dinner on full display. Rita didn't respond in kind, but she also didn't want to get mad or make a scene. Instead, she focused on putting her mask on and then, without a word, walked toward the exit. Rita could hear his footsteps behind her along with some fumbling, which she presumed to be Raj taking out and reattaching his mask.

"Where are you parked?" he asked when they reached the sidewalk. "I'll escort you to your car."

Rita pointed toward her Audi A4.

"I had a wonderful evening. I'd love to see you again," Raj said as they approached her car. She looked away momentarily.

Raj seems to have a good heart. Two hours flew by. That's always a good sign. I've picked up on some red flags, but why not give him a second chance?

"That's a great idea," she said while unlocking her driver's-side door. Rita stepped into the car, closed the door, and rolled down her window. She didn't want him to attempt another farewell move.

"Call or text, and we'll figure it out. Thanks again. Night!" She waved and drove off.

A text from Raj thanking her for a wonderful evening arrived soon after she got home. She thanked him again in her reply. Rita also wrote that although she appreciated his gesture, she wasn't comfortable kissing him until she'd gotten to know him a lot better.

He texted back immediately. "*I understand. I can wait.*"

The Rest of the Story

Raj texted Rita the next day to arrange their second date. It was set for the following week. This time, Raj chose the restaurant, and he once again came to Rita's neighborhood. When he offered to pick her up, she told him she'd prefer to meet at the restaurant. Raj was already seated at an outdoor table when Rita arrived. With him were a small floral arrangement and a bag of M&M's. After Rita sat down, they both removed their masks. As on their first date, Raj lavished her with compliments and spoke about activities he foresaw them doing together. Rita felt smothered.

Upon reaching her car after they'd finished their meal, Raj asked Rita if she was going to miss him. She wasn't sure if he was kidding. Even if he was, Raj was coming on too strong for her and acting overly needy.

The text she received from him that night thanked her for another wonderful evening. Rita texted him back.

"*Thanks again for dinner. I'm glad we had the chance to meet. After some consideration, I don't think we're a good match. I wish you the best.*"

Rita didn't hear from Raj again.

Dating Takeaway Tips

DIFFERENT ISN'T WRONG.

We all have expectations that we've set for ourselves and for others, whether we realize it or not. There are things that you expect to be done a certain way and are disappointed, possibly even troubled, when they aren't. That doesn't mean that what's happened is bad or wrong; it's just different. It's best to try to look deeper, to tease out the reason behind what transpired before drawing conclusions.

Rita's expectation was that her date would select the restaurant. When Raj asked her to do it, she was disappointed and took his request to mean that he didn't want to spend time planning for her date, which meant that he didn't value her. She let his failure to meet her unstated expectation briefly diminish her self-worth. Rita didn't realize that Raj had shifted the choice of restaurant to her because he wanted her to feel safe when they met. It was important to him that she be in a surrounding that was comfortable for her. What Raj did wasn't wrong. It was actually thoughtful. But it didn't correspond with what Rita thought she wanted, and she didn't take the time to look at things from his perspective before drawing her conclusion.

CONSIDER GIVING THEM A SECOND CHANCE.

You might write off someone based on how things went on the first date when in fact the two of you could be a match. The pressure that comes with meeting someone new can cause any of us to be off our game. Start out by giving your date the benefit of the doubt and recognize that everyone has their own style. Unbeknownst to you, your date could be anxious about being at their best in order to impress you. Dating is about discovery. If you sense a connection, and your safety isn't at risk, consider giving that person a second chance. In doing so, you'll never look back and wonder "what if," and you might even realize that your first impression was wrong.

Rita was open to exploring whether she and Raj were compatible. Although she had her reservations, Rita agreed to a second date because she found him to be nice and kind. She also gave herself permission to speak up about being uncomfortable with their interactions. Rita ended the dating process with Raj after she was sure he wasn't right for her. At least she could never question whether she'd said goodbye to him too soon.

SET CLEAR BOUNDARIES

Boundaries are present in all our relationships, be it with family members, colleagues, friends, or romantic partners. Your boundaries declare what it is you need to feel safe and protected, what you will and won't do, and the actions and behaviors you will and won't accept from others. These demarcations establish how you expect to be treated.

When you compromise your boundaries to seek someone's approval, or because of concerns for how they'll react to your pushback, you start to walk down a slippery slope. By surrendering your boundary lines, you begin to forgo what's important to you in favor of what's important to someone else. This can impact your security, self-worth, and mental health.

Telling your date about your boundaries before meeting for

the first time probably wasn't as common as it became once the global pandemic hit. Concerns about contracting Covid-19 got many prospective daters talking about what they would and wouldn't agree to do so they'd avoid contracting the virus. Boundaries involving masking, touching, and maintaining distance were suddenly thrust into early conversations. People adapted. Maybe you've had this experience?

Raj and Rita had just this type of conversation before their debut date. But then he crossed Rita's boundary when he unexpectedly kissed her in the middle of the café. Although at the moment when it happened Rita didn't express to Raj that he'd violated her boundaries, she let him know later by text. From the response he sent, it was clear that Raj respected her and would adhere to the boundaries that she had put in place. When you feel it's time to share your boundaries with your date, do so. If they don't oblige, then they probably are not the right person for you.

"Daring to set boundaries is about having the courage to love ourselves, even when we risk disappointing others."

— Brené Brown, PhD, LMSW
author and professor

The Traffic Trifecta

(A note from Jodi: This is the story about how I met my husband and our debut date.)

I don't like to be late for first dates. But there I sat in my motionless car, boxed in behind a minivan, with a Toyota Prius to my right trying to inch into my lane, an immobile bright cobalt-blue BMW to my left, and a red truck creeping uncomfortably close to my rear bumper. The one-way, three-lane street on which I was trapped was lined with vehicles going nowhere. Time was moving forward, but we weren't. The traffic jam was worse than any I'd experienced on the streets of San Francisco.

Michael had suggested we meet at a café on the southern side of town. He'd merely have to walk a few blocks, while I'd need to travel all the way across the city.

There were an unusual number of major civic events taking place that weekend, but I'd agreed to meet him at the far-off location.

Why not? I thought. *I've been driving on these streets since I got my license. I know my way around this town better than most.*

Being the planner that I am, I did the driving calculus to figure out how much extra time I'd need to give myself. I had added twenty minutes for possible traffic slowdowns triggered by a street closure due to a big tech conference, and fifteen minutes for delays that the thousands of Navy sailors descending on the city for the upcoming Fleet Week festivities might cause. My early departure would have me pulling into a parking space close to the café with enough time to scan my phone for any pressing texts, apply a new coat of lipstick, and casually walk inside. Or so I'd thought.

That I had to get back to my neighborhood in time for a family dinner that evening hadn't been a concern. I certainly wasn't going to miss my birthday celebration, even if it was two days premature. I had been sure I could do the round trip and have a sufficient amount of time for a long enough conversation with Michael to learn more about him. We were meeting for coffee, after all. It was my MO to spend an hour, tops, on coffee dates, and only if I found the guy interesting and attractive.

The "attractive box" had been checked. He'd seemed interesting, too, but we'd spoken so briefly that I couldn't be sure. Maybe it didn't even matter. The wording of Michael's e-mail had left me wondering if he'd asked me out on a date or if he was just looking to do some business networking. I was hoping for the former.

It was 2:55 p.m. Michael would be arriving at the café in five minutes. He needed to know I wouldn't be there to greet him.

"*I'm SO sorry!*" I texted. "*I'm trapped in nightmare traffic. I'm going to be late.*"

He texted back immediately. "*No problem. I'll wait.*"

Three days earlier I'd attended a networking event for local politicians and businesspeople. I squarely fell into the latter category. Walking through the doors of the Intercontinental Hotel that Tuesday night, I didn't know if I'd be navigating the room alone or with friends. Peggy and Eric had texted me a few days earlier. Both were unsure whether they'd make it and hadn't RSVPed yet. When I scanned the sea of unclaimed name tags laid out on the reception table and didn't see theirs, I knew I'd be solo that night.

The e-mail invitation had arrived in my inbox two months earlier. Without a crystal ball, it would have been impossible for the organizers to predict that their invitees would have to choose between their event and watching the San Francisco Giants play the Washington Nationals for the National League Division Series title on TV that evening.

The city was abuzz with baseball playoff fever. I'd been infected like so many others. I'd probably have no-showed the event as well, had one of the featured speakers not been a politician who'd introduced legislation to the board of supervisors that I opposed. I didn't want to pass up a rare opportunity to have easy access to the supervisor to give him input about how he could improve his bill. When a friend invited me to her baseball game–watching party that night, I told her I'd come, but late. I loved watching a game live, but DVRs were created for a reason.

Stepping onto the hotel's long, narrow terrace, I surveyed the scene. The spacious room was only a quarter full, at best. The people who'd stayed true to their "yes" RSVPs were mostly standing along the side walls chatting in groups of twos and threes. No one looked familiar to me.

Mostly unused high-top tables ran down the center of the room. At one, a tall man in a dark blue suit stood alone. His back was to me. From its curvature, I could tell he was eating.

My many years of business networking had taught me that starting a conversation with one stranger was monumentally easier than injecting myself into a group of strangers already chatting away. The official remarks likely wouldn't start for at least thirty minutes. I needed someone to talk to until then, so I started walking toward him. I was four feet away when he stepped from the table and headed for the buffet. I did the only sensible thing that a woman in need of both food and a networking companion could do—I followed him. Once at the food table, I picked up a plate and slid in line behind him.

His back remained to me. We inched along, past the platter of sliced vegetables and hummus. I waited for an opportunity to arise for me to say something. It was when he picked a chicken skewer off a tray and dipped it in sauce that I saw my opening.

"Does that dip look spicy to you?" I asked, leaning slightly into his personal space. He turned to his left, greeted me with a warm smile, and looked down at the sauce on his plate.

"I don't think it is, but let me find out." He took a bite of the chicken. "No, it's not spicy," he said with a reassuring voice. I smiled, impressed that this man I'd just met had gone beyond a cavalier "I don't know" response.

"I'm a self-confessed spice wimp. I really appreciate you being my food taster," I said with a smile before placing two sauce-dipped skewers on my plate. "I'm Jodi."

"Nice to meet you. I'm Michael."

We conversed about the array of food as we moved along the line. At the roast beef station, the buffet's grand finale, the caterer placed two pristinely sliced pieces of roast beef on his plate. "Would you like to join me at one of the tables?" Michael asked.

"Sure, that would be great!" My smile widened. I did cartwheels inside.

After a brief detour to the bar, I joined Michael at a high-top table with a glass of red wine in one hand and the plate of hors d'oeuvres in the other.

"What do you do?" he asked before taking a bite of a hummus-covered carrot. I talked about running a marketing consulting firm. He told me he did business development for a financial lending company.

As Michael spoke, I took in his thick and lustrous salt-and-pepper hair. He had youthful skin, sculpted cheekbones, and a sharp jawline. His gorgeous hazel eyes were framed by gentle crow's feet below and a graceful brow above. He looked like a cross between Cary Grant and Charlie Sheen.

Michael is too good-looking, and seemingly normal, for a woman not to have claimed him. I've already gone on a lunch date today anyway, so I've met my quota.

I ate a slice of bell pepper as I listened to Michael talk about the start-up where he worked. His voice had a slightly atypical cadence to it.

I'm detecting an accent; he pronounces his r's differently, his e's are softer, and he puts more of an emphasis on the last syllable of words.

Michael took a sip of wine.

"You weren't born in the US, were you?" I asked in as nonchalant a manner as I knew how. He chuckled as he returned the glass to the table. If I'd caught him off guard, he didn't show it.

"You're right. I wasn't." Michael placed his hand over his name tag. "Where do you think I'm from? No cheating," he said with a deep-throated laugh.

I thought about it for a few moments. "Hmmm, you're from France." My tone of voice conveyed more confidence in my conclusion than I actually felt.

"Très bien!" Michael said, raising his glass again. I clinked his with mine, and we both took sips. "I was born and raised in Paris, but I've lived in the States for almost half my life. Have you been to Paris?"

I told him I had, but that it'd been over a decade since I'd last visited the City of Lights. We discovered we shared a love for travel. Our conversation wound its way from traveling in Europe, to traveling around the US, to travel for work.

"I used to fly a lot for work, but that was years ago," I said. "I don't miss it. Flying isn't nearly as enjoyable in this post-9/11 world we live in." I paused to finish off the remaining piece of roast beef that sat abandoned on my plate.

"So, what's your relationship status?" he asked. The out-of-the-blue question was delivered in a casual manner, the kind you use when asking what the weather is like, or where the restroom is. But there was nothing casual about it. My head lurched forward, briefly lodging the piece of meat that I was halfway through swallowing in my throat. A few coughs, followed by some red wine, and I'd recovered my composure.

"I'm single . . . but dating," I responded, pausing midsentence to decide how to sum up the state of my love life after twenty-six years of singledom.

"Good to know," he said.

I'd been certain that a man as handsome as he was would be married. As Michael tipped his head back to finish off the remaining wine in his glass, I surreptitiously glanced at his ring finger. It was bare.

"I'm going to the bar to get something else to drink," he said. "I'll be right back."

I gazed down into my glass. Holding the base of the stem, I gently rotated it and watched the remaining burgundy liquid slosh in circles.

I didn't see that coming! Do I want to get to know him better? Heck yes!

"Ahem," I heard coming from behind me. I turned around to see Michael there but without a second glass of wine. "I have to leave. Do you have a business card?"

"Uh . . . sure, yes, I do." I fumbled through my purse, extracted one from its scratched silver case, and handed it to him.

"Thanks. I completely lost track of time. I have another dinner to go to. Here's mine." I took his card without looking down, my eyes fixed on his. In them I saw honesty and kindness.

"It was very nice meeting you. Bye."

My slightly confused gaze remained on Michael as he retreated to the opposite side of the room and disappeared through the doorway.

What just happened? He asked me if I was single and then he bolted.

My contemplation was interrupted by a different male voice

to my right. "Hello." Next to me stood a gray-haired man, about my height, wearing a brown corduroy jacket. His disheveled hair and unkempt beard desperately needed attending to by a barber.

"I'm Fred. What do you do?" he asked. I answered briefly and kept the conversation high-level, anticipating that the evening's speakers would address the attendees soon. As if on cue, the event host welcomed everyone from the podium, and the formal remarks began.

Thanks to the event's low attendance, I didn't have to wade through a crowd of people to speak to the city supervisor after the speeches ended. I told him why I thought he should change his legislation. He nodded and assured me that the restrictions I was concerned about had been removed. With my mission accomplished, I left the hotel and headed to my friend's baseball watching party. Driving to her apartment, I replayed what had happened with Michael.

His question about my relationship status was so unexpected. And then he left abruptly. Am I going to hear from the guy again?

I didn't have to wait long for the answer. It came the next afternoon in the form of a LinkedIn e-mail.

Hi Jodi,

Nice meeting you at the networking event. Sorry I couldn't stay longer. Let me know if you are up for coffee later this week. Would love to hear more about your diverse activities! I'd like to add you to my professional network on LinkedIn.

—Michael

The excitement that streaked through me like a comet left bewilderment in its wake.

Why did he e-mail me through LinkedIn? He has my cell number and e-mail address. Is he asking me to a business meeting or on a date?

I sat at my laptop, my fingers impatiently resting on the keyboard as I mulled over my response. What I wrote needed to be warm and receptive but not overly enthusiastic in case he was just asking me to a business coffee.

> *Hi Michael,*
>
> *It was nice to meet you at the event too. Sure, I'm up for coffee. This week I can do Friday at 3 pm or 4 pm. Does either time work for you?*
>
> *Cheers, Jodi*

LinkedIn delivered his reply a few hours later. We were on for Friday at three. I'd only have to wait a few days to discover what his motivations were behind his invite.

I pressed "refresh" on Google Maps. Up popped a map on my phone showing the blue dot that marked my car, moored within a grid of red roads, alleyways, and side streets. The traffic soothsayer was predicting I'd arrive at the café a full hour late! My body wilted. My forehead landed, gently, atop my static steering wheel.

This is so frustrating! What is causing this mess?

Revived by the need to know why I was trapped in gridlock, I spun my car radio's scan dial in search of a news report. It took more than one lap around the AM stations before I heard a traffic reporter's surprising announcement explaining why the northeast part of the city had turned to crimson on my phone.

"Downtown streets, freeway on-ramps and off-ramps, are all closed as President Obama's motorcade moves from the Financial District to South of Market," she said.

The president of the United States is making me late for my date? No way! Add this to Fleet Week and the tech conference, and I'm in the midst of a traffic trifecta!

I chuckled as I texted Michael. *"Obama is downtown. Who knew? This gridlock is worse because of his visit. Again, so sorry!"*

He texted back. *"I had no idea. I'm still okay waiting."*

The cars in front of me had begun to gradually creep forward. It was 3:15. I surveyed the scene. Some drivers were staring out their windshields, their hands tightly gripped on their steering wheels, their knuckles likely turning white. Others sat back in their seats, having rolled down their windows to welcome the warm autumn evening breeze. Music and conversation emanated from the cars closest to me. A few were bumper to bumper, though I noticed most had a few feet of space between them.

If Michael's going to wait, I'm not letting the leader of the free world stop me from getting to that café!

"I'm going to maneuver out of this traffic. I'll be there. My apologies," I texted.

"Great. Reading the paper," he texted back.

I turned the steering wheel tightly to the right and began

inching my way into the adjacent lane. As the Prius gradually slipped into the gap that was opening in front of my car, I maneuvered to the right to fill the space it had surrendered.

The president, and the gridlock that his visit had generated, were in the east end of the city. Unfortunately, so was Michael. But the café was a few blocks south of the worst of the traffic. I resolved to drive west until I got behind the gridlock. Upon reaching the rear of it, I'd cross Market Street to enter on the south side of town and attempt to drive east. Whenever I came across a line of backed-up cars, I'd turn onto a southbound street, zigzagging my way to Crossroads Café.

My strategy worked. I steered the car onto less congested roads, instinctively making sharp right and left turns onto main streets and down alleyways. It was as though I was channeling a slower version of Steve McQueen in *Bullitt*.

The phone rang. It was my dad. "I remember you saying you are going to be in the South of Market area. Your mom's downtown. Can you pick her up on your way across the city?"

She had returned that afternoon from a three-day getaway to Lake Tahoe with some friends and had been dropped off at one of their apartments. My mom had three transportation options to get to the birthday dinner: a taxi, a rideshare, or me.

"No problem," I told my father as I drove down a one-way side street. "I'll be less than a mile from her." *Presuming I ever get there.*

I hung up not knowing if the drive to pick her up would take the typical amount of time or turn out to be a half-hour-long slog. Still, it was my mom. I wasn't going to have her take an Uber. I'd need to plan for forty minutes at the café, leaving me even less time to spend with Michael.

When I was three blocks from the café, I spotted a parking spot. Knowing that spaces in that neighborhood can be hard to find, I opted to surrender my car and do the rest of the trip on foot. It was 3:42.

I leaped out of the car, purse and jacket in hand, and did my best to jog in heels. I rushed through crosswalks, hopped onto curbs, and scurried down sidewalks to the sounds of honking in the distance. The traffic was still ensnarled.

It was with the exhilaration of a marathon runner breaking through the finish-line tape that I burst through the café's door. I took a few deep breaths to lower my racing heartbeat and looked around. Michael wasn't seated at the wooden tables or in one of the oversized lounge chairs. Could he have left? I was relieved to notice a doorway to my right that led outside. I walked through it and onto a brick patio.

The outdoor space was serene. Trees shaded the tables and the laced ironwork–backed chairs placed around them. The elegant maples, with their deep burgundy leaves, were rooted in large flower-lined planters along the south side of the patio. Running the length of the north side was a thick soundproof wall that successfully held the noise of the traffic chaos at bay.

I saw a tall man seated at a table in the middle of the patio. The newspaper he was reading obscured his face but not his salt-and-pepper hair that peeked above it. I hurried over.

"Hi! I am *so* sorry that I'm incredibly late!" I said.

The paper lowered, and Michael's friendly hazel eyes greeted me.

"It wasn't a problem. It's a gorgeous fall day, and I found some newspapers to read." Michael stood up. He was taller than

I'd remembered. At five foot eight, I stood eye to eye, or slightly above, many of the men I dated. But not Michael. He was at least six feet tall.

"I feel bad that you had to deal with that traffic jam to get here. It was very nice of you to keep me posted. Please sit down," he said, gesturing to the empty chair.

"Can you believe that President Obama almost came between us?" I asked in jest while placing my purse on the table. "I knew about the tech conference and Fleet Week, but I had no idea I'd have to keep tabs on the president's travel plans to get to you on time." We laughed. I liked the way his eyes sparkled.

"I'll go get you a drink. What would you like? Coffee? Tea? Something else?"

He headed into the café after I selected tea.

I sat down, exhaled, and marveled at the dramatic contrast between my calm surroundings and the traffic mayhem a few blocks away. I was happy to be with Michael but knew I'd have to keep tabs on the time.

"Here you go. I hope you like green tea." He placed the glass mug with steaming water and submerged tea bag on the table before me. His coffee cup was empty.

"Am I drinking solo?" I asked playfully.

"I'm a one-coffee-a-day man. If I have a cup after four, it keeps me up for most of the night. Does that happen to you too?"

"This will likely come as a surprise to a Frenchman, but I don't drink coffee."

"You what? Don't drink coffee? How can this be?" Michael looked at me as though I'd just told him that pigs can fly. "Have you *ever* had coffee?"

"Yes. Once. I didn't love it. And I don't need all that caffeine. Tea's more my thing."

I sipped some of the tea, and from there the conversation dovetailed into other types of hot beverages we did and didn't like.

"My favorite is a Hot Peppermint Patty after a full day of skiing. Peppermint schnapps, crème de cacao, and hot chocolate topped off with whipped cream—delish! There's no more satisfying drink after tearing up the slopes."

"Ah, you're a skier?" Michael asked, leaning in slightly. "I am too. It's my second favorite sport. Squash is my first."

From that springboard, we plunged into an animated recounting of our skiing adventures. We discovered that we both had our parents to thank for introducing us to the sport when we were five. He told me about Chamonix, Val-d'Isère, and other European ski resorts he'd been to that I had never heard of before. I told him about one of my earliest memories of being pulled out of a ditch at the base of a soaring pine tree at the end of my dad's ski pole after I accidentally slid off a rope tow. Michael's eyes lit up as he spoke about introducing his now grown son and daughter to Squaw Valley for the first time when they were in elementary school. They took to the sport right away. Years of skiing together followed. Michael and I'd already uncovered a shared passion.

I also learned that we almost didn't meet on Tuesday.

"The business dinner I left you to go to was arranged a few weeks after I'd registered for the networking event. I almost went straight to the dinner. That would have been a huge mistake!" He smiled widely.

I looked down at my cup and began fiddling with the tea bag's string, a convenient decoy. Had he noticed that I was blushing? After waiting a few moments to give the color time to recede, I took a sip and looked at Michael. My lips formed a smile that mirrored his.

"Good thing you're a man of your word," I said teasingly.

Our repartee resumed its light banter as we moved on to other topics. Michael asked lots of questions. He made jokes. Most of them I got and thought were funny, but I laughed at them all. I was comfortable in his company. Talking to him was easy. He mentioned he'd been divorced for over ten years. He gave me an introductory primer on squash, and we chatted about how I love to dance. The time flew by, and when I glanced at my watch, I realized forty-five minutes had passed. I told him about my evening's upcoming plans.

"I'm so sorry, but I'd better get going," I said. "I shouldn't be late for the dinner reservation, and I don't want to keep my mom waiting."

"Not a problem. I completely understand."

I collected my jacket and purse, picked up my empty teacup, and we headed back into the café.

After we deposited our dirty cups in the cleaning bin, we stood silently facing each other. It was the first time I'd felt any awkwardness between us. Or was it something else?

Since he had not mentioned a second date, I deployed my go-to line that I'd say to men who I wanted to see again but who had not expressed the same yet.

"I had a nice time. If you want to get together again, let me know."

"Yes, let's do that," he said, smiling. He moved in for a hug. I could feel the strength in his arms as he wrapped them around me. I fit perfectly in his embrace; my head would have rested at the top of his chest if ours had been an intimate hug and not the "nice to meet you" kind. I tilted my head back and looked up at him with a smile of my own. Our hug lasted for no more than a few seconds, but it still felt comfortable.

"And," he continued afterward, "have a great birthday this weekend. I'll be in touch."

The Rest of the Story

The traffic had eased up a little while I was drinking tea with Michael. Earlier in the day, I'd told my mom about my plans to meet with him and that I wasn't sure if I was going on a date. The first thing she asked after she got into my car was, "Was it a date or a business meeting?"

"It was a date."

"How do you know?"

"Because he didn't ask me one question about business!" We burst out laughing as I drove us to the restaurant.

Two days later, Michael texted to wish me well on my birthday. The texting resumed the following night while I was at a bar with friends watching Monday Night Football and he was traveling for work. Our flirtatious back-and-forth culminated with his asking me out for a drink on Friday night. There was no confusion this time. We were going on a date.

The drink that I'd expected would take one to two hours

morphed into five hours of wandering and exploring the streets of San Francisco together. After we left the bar, we went for a walk, spontaneously stopped at an Italian restaurant for dinner, strolled some more, popped into a small ice cream shop, and meandered around until the moment when our first kiss happened—while standing in front of a strip club, of all places.

Our courtship moved at a fast pace. Within a month Michael had met my parents and soon after was introduced to the entire local family at Thanksgiving dinner. We started taking trips, spending time with each other's friends, opening up to each other about life's challenges and our hopes for the future. The deeper we delved, the tighter our bond grew, and with it, our love. Michael proposed on the ten-month anniversary of the day we met. I couldn't have been more surprised, not only because he proposed in French (a language I didn't understand) but because we hadn't yet discussed marriage. We got married eleven months later, making me a first-time bride at the age of forty-nine.

Dating Takeaway Tips

GO TO SOCIAL EVENTS ALONE.

Though the prospect of going out solo might make you nervous, if you want to meet new people, one of the best ways is to be your own date. Have you declined invitations because you didn't have a friend to walk into the room with? It's understandable, but you're working against your own self-interest of meeting new people.

Reverse your thinking. It may feel uncomfortable to mill around alone in a room of people who are busy socializing. But at the same time, you don't have a physical barrier—that friend or colleague—beside you unintentionally blocking someone else from approaching. It's less intimidating for someone new to come up to you when you're alone, not to mention that you'll also force yourself to walk up to others. I would never have met Michael if my two friends had been at the Intercontinental Hotel that evening. They did me a favor. Do yourself a favor and say yes to events where you'll know no one.

TALK TO STRANGERS

Have you ever spotted someone from across the room and immediately wanted to meet them, but you weren't sure what to say or do, so you didn't do anything? It's so easy to miss these opportunities—these gifts—to connect with others. You lose out on saying hello to someone new who might add something special to your life, and they've been denied the chance to get to know you, even a little.

For a conversation to start, two things must happen. First, you must conquer any reticence or fear you have to approach and talk to a stranger. Secondly, the stranger needs to be receptive to speaking to someone they don't know. Since you are only in control of your own actions, don't take it personally if they don't eagerly engage. You don't know their story or what they might be going through.

Need a few pointers on how to avoid awkward small talk and get a friendly conversation going? The easiest way is to start by asking questions. Most people love talking about themselves.

It's easy. After all, it's the topic we all know most about. And you're signaling that you're interested in them. They'll likely be flattered and more apt to let their guard down, at least a bit.

Try these steps after someone's caught your eye:

1. Take a breath. The more relaxed you are, the more relaxed they will be. People pick up on our cues.

2. Approach them with a genuine smile and say, "Hi." Keep your eyes focused on them. Don't let your eyes dart around the room.

3. Comment on something related to what they're doing (such as asking a question about the book they're reading on the bus), compliment them in some way ("Hey, I see you're rooting for _____. You know how to pick a great team!"), or ask a question about them ("I like your Rolling Stones T-shirt. Have you seen the band perform live?"). You can also make a joke about what's going on around you or what that person is up to at that moment ("I see you've got two glasses of beer. Double-fisting, huh?"). Humor has a way of dispelling discomfort for both people, unless it's criticism disguised as a joke.

    No pickup lines allowed, and don't worry about flirting. You can do it later. The point here is to put them at ease and encourage them to open up to you.

4. If they engage, let the conversation flow naturally. If they don't, move on with confidence—it isn't you, it's them.

If the conversation quickly peters out, end it by saying something like, "It's been really nice chatting with you. Enjoy the rest of your day." Don't get down or be self-critical. It's natural that we don't connect with everybody. Remind yourself that you are confident, worthy, and it's their loss that they didn't engage. It's all good!

One day, you may start a conversation with a stranger who becomes a new friend or, possibly, your new love. Whatever happens, you're taking steps toward expanding your horizons, learning and growing with each encounter. Way to go!

"Love is the emblem of eternity;
it confounds all notion of time,
effaces all memory of beginning, all fear of an end."

— *Madame de Staël*
author and political intellectual

The Rest of Your Story

"**Y**ou've got to *keep* showing up."

I often heard that maxim during my childhood. My father would dispense his encouraging words when I was dragging my feet, reluctant to follow through on a commitment or to try something new.

They were said to me when I refused to go to my shift working the Girl Scout cookie stand in front of the local grocery store the day after I'd missed my cookie-selling target by a mile. (You'd think the Samoa and Thin Mint cookies would practically sell themselves.) My father recited those words when I was worried I wouldn't do well on a middle school science test, after I'd lost an election in high school, and again, and again.

By the time I'd graduated college, his motto had been engrained in me. It had become my own. The principle makes sense. We should each be actively present in our own lives to help make our dreams a reality, and to grow as individuals when things don't work out as we'd hoped they would.

My father never intended for those words to apply to dating, but they do. A friend who's in her early fifties lives by the same principle. Taylor is a lovely, athletic, accomplished businesswoman who's never been married. She'd like to meet a lifelong partner. For her, each date is as much an opportunity to learn about the man she's meeting as it is a chance to widen her horizons through the new ideas or subject matters he may share. Taylor shows up to find love, as well as to expand and grow as a person. She focuses on being present for the present.

So did the women whose stories are in this book. They learned from what they lived. Take the lessons from their tales to heart. Continue to create your own new first date stories— even with men who may not seem like your ideal fit—until you meet the one who is deserving of you and who loves, cherishes, and respects you for the fabulous woman you are. If that day does not arrive, keep your self-love tank full. Believe that you are enough, because you are. You are complete without a partner.

Remember that you are not alone on this journey. Have faith in the process. Use online dating sites, dating apps, virtual dating, and expand your horizons offline to meet new men and make new girlfriends. Grow your social network. Try activities you've never attempted before. Book your calendar with a wide variety of events. Be brave and do things solo. Take breaks from dating when you need to. Then get back on the first date roller coaster and enjoy the ride.

Gratitude

This book wouldn't be in your hands, or on your device, had it not been for the women who entrusted me to tell their dating stories. I thank each of you wonderful women for generously contributing a memorable vignette from your lives to this collection. You recognized the power of storytelling and its potent ability to entertain, comfort, and provide guidance to others. It's been an honor to do my best to capture your tales and derive teachings from your experiences.

These women's accounts of their unforgettable first dates would likely have remained in my notebook, and not made it into short-story form, were it not for the Dueling Pens: Marina Broido, Marguerite Hanley, and Garrett Miller. Our monthly meetings over beef and veggie burgers and the wickedest of sweet potato fries, where we shared writing exercises and workshopped each other's compositions, were challenging, invigorating, and fun. Marina, Marguerite, and Garrett, your no-holds-barred critiques of most of the stories in this book substantially improved the drafts, as well as my craft. Over seven years, you helped me build confidence in my prose and bolstered my belief that I had a message to share that was worthy of this book's publication. Special kudos to you, Garrett, for suggesting the use of quotations to transition between the stories. I'm immensely grateful to each of you and continue to be motivated by our dissolved writing group's rallying cry—Write on!

What a delight it was to have love and relationship coach Sarika Jain fine-tune this book's dating takeaway tips. Your soulful guidance and joy-filled approach to life make it clear why you're known as the Relationship Sorceress.

Thanks and credit go to Jennifer Wexler. The story you kindly sourced for me soon after we met put the finishing touch on this collection.

To my copyeditor, Angie Frazier, thank you for working with me through multiple rounds of revisions. You made the manuscript glisten.

Many thanks to Karen Nelson for her magnanimous guidance. Whenever I had a writing or industry-related question, and I had many, you always responded with a helpful answer that moved me further down the path toward publishing.

I've been blessed with a treasure chest full of magnificent friends. You've all cheered me on as I've sought to bring the *First Date Stories* initiative to single women in midlife everywhere. From the time I conceived of the idea, to the launch of the podcast and blog, to the publication of this book, you've been on this journey with me. An immense thanks to each of you for listening when I've shared my challenges and frustrations, dispensing sage advice, making introductions I've requested along the way, and high-fiving when there have been milestones to celebrate. I cherish you all. You're proof positive that friendship is one of life's greatest gifts.

How fortunate I am that my close friend Shana Daum has also been my media guru and confidante. You believed in me and this project from its inception. Your steadfast support has been priceless!

To my dear friend and trusted sounding board Jennifer Nock, I'll always appreciate your extraordinary listening skills, sage advice, and infectious giggle. By helping me bat away occasional doubts that crept in, you enabled me to stay true to my goal of publishing this book. I hold your memory close to my heart and think about you every day.

Mom and Dad, my boundless gratitude to you both goes well beyond the publication of this book. I lucked out on the parents lottery. Your unconditional love and belief that I can achieve whatever I set out to accomplish have added fuel to my fire and propelled me forward since I was a little girl. Dad, you are the definition of the American dream. From you, I've learned an immeasurable amount about being a good person, why laughter is the best medicine, and how to be an avid football fan. Mom, you've been a strong female role model and a pioneer on many fronts. I stand up for myself and for what I believe in because you showed me how. Your insatiable love of learning and community has been infectious. Thank you for regularly checking in on how this venture is going and for being an evangelist for it.

To my "Mr. Yes," Michael Darnaud, you have my heart and my unending love. *Un grand merci* for your unwavering support of my dream to publish this book. I wake up every day feeling blessed to be by your side. I love the life we've created together, *mon amour*, and I feel like the luckiest woman on planet Earth. You were absolutely worth the wait.

SELECTED TITLES FROM SHE WRITES PRESS

She Writes Press is an independent publishing company
founded to serve women writers everywhere.
Visit us at www.shewritespress.com.

Daring to Date Again: A Memoir by Ann Anderson Evans. $16.95,
978-1-63152-909-2. A hilarious, no-holds-barred memoir about a
legal secretary turned professor who dives back into the dating pool
headfirst after twelve years of celibacy.

Broken Whole: A Memoir by Jane Binns. $16.95, 978-1-63152-433-2.
At the age of thirty-five, desperate to salvage a self that has been
suffocating for years, Jane Binns leaves her husband of twelve years.
She has no plan or intention but to leave, however—and there begin
the misadventures lying in wait for her.

Insatiable: A Memoir of Love Addiction by Shary Hauer. $16.95,
978-1-63152-982-5. An intimate and illuminating account of
corporate executive—and secret love addict—Shary Hauer's
migration from destructive to healthy love.

Miracle at Midlife: A Transatlantic Romance by Roni Beth Tower.
$16.95, 978-1-63152-123-2. An inspiring memoir chronicling the
sudden, unexpected, and life-changing two-year courtship between a
divorced American lawyer living on a houseboat in the center of Paris
and an empty-nested clinical psychologist living in Connecticut.

Not a Perfect Fit: Stories from Jane's World by Jane A. Schmidt. $16.95,
978-1631522062. Jane Schmidt documents her challenges living off
the grid, moving from the city to the country, living with a variety of
animals as her only companions, dating, family trips, outdoor
adventures, and midlife in essays full of honesty and humor.

Erotic Integrity: How to be True to Yourself Sexually by Claudia Six,
PhD. $16.95, 978-1-63152-079-2. Dr. Claudia Six, a respected clinical
sexologist and relationship coach, presents her unique method to
uncovering your true sexual desires and attaining a more authentic
and satisfying sexuality.

About the Author

Photo credit: Laura Reoch

Jodi Klein knows what it's like to date longer and later in life. A demanding career and desire to find her "Mr. Yes" led to her becoming an alumna of nearly four hundred dates over the course of twenty-six years. She founded *First Date Stories*— the podcast and the blog—as a platform for women to share their tales and wisdom so that others can overcome the trials of dating in midlife and find the long-term love they seek. Jodi is an entrepreneur, a marketing executive with over two decades of high-tech experience, a real estate broker, and the president of Espoir Ventures, LLC. She is a graduate of UC Davis and holds an MBA from the Ross School of Business at the University of Michigan. Jodi lives with her husband in San Francisco, where she spends time working with non-profits on social causes and rooting for her favorite sports teams. For more information, please visit JodiKlein.com.